Grief and Loss in the Age of AI

Talking to the Dead and Coping With Loss in a Digital World

Sera Vale

Imperium Ink

GRIEF AND LOSS in the age of AI

Talking to the Dead and Coping With Loss in a Digital World

Sera Vale

Disclaimer

This book is intended for general information and education. It reflects the author's research and understanding at the time of publication. Digital technologies, platform policies, and legal frameworks change quickly, and readers should be aware that information may become outdated or may not apply in every location.

Nothing in this book should be taken as legal, financial, psychological, therapeutic, or professional advice. Readers should seek independent guidance from qualified professionals before making decisions about digital estate planning, grief support, data management, or any other matter discussed in these pages.

The author and publisher accept no responsibility for any loss, harm, or consequences that may arise from the use or misuse of the information in this book. This includes emotional, financial, legal, or practical outcomes. The author cannot be held liable for actions taken by readers or for any interpretations or assumptions made from the content.

Some topics in this book may be sensitive or confronting. They are presented in good faith and are not intended to cause distress or offence. Every reader's circumstances and values are unique, and the ideas in this book should be adapted to individual needs and contexts.

By reading this book, you acknowledge that you do so voluntarily and that you accept full responsibility for your choices and actions.

First Edition, 2026

Published by Imperium Ink

ISBN: 978-1-7644347-3-7

For my mother, whose memory guided my hand,
and whose voice I still carry within me.

Contents

Introduction

When my colleague's father died, she said she found herself returning to the small digital traces he had left behind. One evening, while sorting through her phone, she opened a long thread of their text messages. Years of everyday conversations appeared on the screen. Weather updates. Quick questions. Reminders about groceries. The kind of exchanges that feel forgettable when life is ordinary but become immeasurably precious once someone is gone. She told me she read through them slowly, almost afraid to reach the end, because each message felt like a moment she had somehow been given back.

As she sat with those memories, she remembered a friend had mentioned a new AI service that could recreate a person's texting style and generate fresh conversations based on their old messages. The idea unsettled her and intrigued her in equal measure. She asked what I thought of it. I realised I did not have an answer. Not because the technology was unfamiliar, but because the question she was really asking had no precedent. What does it mean to continue a conversation with someone who is no longer alive? What does it mean to want to?

That moment stayed with me. It marked the first time I understood how profoundly grief is being reshaped by the digital world we now inhabit. We are surrounded by the voices, images, and words of the people we love long after they are gone, and for the first time in history those traces can be made to speak back.

I remembered our conversation not because it was unusual, but because it was becoming increasingly common. We are living through a moment when technology has outpaced our collective understanding of how to grieve. The tools available to process loss have transformed dramatically, yet the ache of bereavement remains as timeless and universal as it has always been.

Today, people may encounter AI grief companions, digital memorials, and technologies that promise continued connection with deceased loved ones, often without clear guidance about whether these tools support healing or complicate it.

This book exists because grief in the digital age requires new frameworks for understanding. Your complicated feelings about using technology in grief are valid. They are also completely normal. The questions you are asking yourself about whether to engage with a digital version of someone you have lost, about what it means to honor memory in an era of artificial intelligence, about how to maintain authentic connection while navigating technological innovation. These are not questions with simple answers. They require honest exploration grounded in both clinical grief science and deep respect for the emotional complexity of bereavement.

What you will find in these pages is not a prescription for how you should grieve, but a research-informed guide to help you make decisions that align with your values, your emotional needs, and your own experience of grief. We will explore what digital loved ones actually are, how they work, and why they can feel emotionally powerful despite being simulations. We will examine the science of grief itself, moving beyond outdated stage models to understand how healthy bereavement involves both confronting loss and maintaining continuing bonds. We will investigate the psychological mechanisms that enable us to form connections with artificial entities, the ethical considerations that arise when we recreate deceased loved ones digitally, and the practical strategies for using these tools safely if you choose to engage with them.

Throughout this exploration, one principle remains central: technology should complement, never replace, the human connections and professional support that remain essential to healthy grief. The BONDS Framework introduced in this book provides a structured, evidence-based approach to evaluating and using digital grief tools, helping you maintain boundaries, honor consent and dignity, protect your psychological wellbeing, and ensure that any technological engagement remains embedded within real-world relationships and support systems.

Perhaps most importantly, this book will help you understand that healing from loss does not mean forgetting. It means integrating memories in constructive ways that allow you to move toward acceptance and meaning-making while still honoring your loved one. Whether you decide in the end whether to use AI grief companions or not, you will finish this book with a clear sense of your own grief patterns, confidence in your decision-making, and agency over your healing.

Grief will continue to evolve as technology advances, but the fundamental human work of learning to live with loss remains unchanged. This book is your companion through that work, offering wisdom, compassion, and practical guidance for navigating bereavement in an age when the boundaries between memory and simulation, between honoring the dead and recreating them, have become more complex than ever before.

Chapter One

Understanding Grief in the Digital Age

"Remembrance of things past is not necessarily the remembrance of things as they were."

Marcel Proust, Remembrance of Things Past

Eliza discovered her mother's voicemail three months after the funeral, saved accidentally in a folder she rarely checked. Hearing that familiar voice - warm, slightly hurried, asking Eliza to pick up milk on the way home, brought an unexpected surge of comfort followed immediately by a wave of fresh grief that left her sitting on her kitchen floor, phone clutched in both hands.

That single voicemail became a touchstone in Eliza's grief journey, but it also raised questions she had never anticipated having to answer. Should she preserve it forever, risking the pain each replay brought? Delete it to avoid the constant reminder?

When a friend mentioned emerging technologies that could use such recordings to create interactive conversations with the deceased, Eliza felt something shift inside her. The possibility of hearing her mother's voice say new things, of receiving comfort and guidance through an algorithm trained on her mother's speech patterns and personality, felt simultaneously like a lifeline and a violation of something sacred she could not quite name.

Eliza's experience reflects a profound transformation in how we navigate loss. Grief itself has not changed. The ache of absence, the disorientation of a world that continues without someone we love, the slow and painful work of learning to live with loss rather than overcome it, these remain as timeless and universal as they have always been. What has changed is the landscape in which grief unfolds. Previous generations mourned with photographs, letters, and memories that existed primarily in the mind and heart. Today's bereaved inherit digital archives of unprecedented depth and detail, from years of text messages and emails to social media profiles that continue to exist long after death, creating what researchers call a persistent digital presence that complicates traditional understandings of how we remember and let go.

The emergence of artificial intelligence has accelerated this transformation dramatically. Technologies that once belonged to science fiction are now commercially available, offering bereaved individuals the possibility of recreating conversations with deceased loved ones through chatbots trained on their digital footprints. These tools promise comfort, connection, and a way to maintain bonds with those we have lost. Yet they also raise profound questions about the nature of grief, the ethics of digital resurrection, and whether technology that feels emotionally powerful actually supports healthy bereavement or complicates it in ways we are only beginning to understand.

This book exists at the intersection of timeless human experience and unprecedented technological capability. It is written for anyone navigating loss in an era where the boundaries between memory and simulation, between honoring the dead and recreating them, have become unexpectedly blurred. Whether you are currently grieving and wondering if AI tools might help, supporting someone who is considering these technologies, or working professionally with bereaved individuals who are encountering digital grief companions, this book offers grounded, research-informed guidance for making sense of this new terrain.

The chapters that follow will explore what digital loved ones are and how they work, why we form emotional bonds with simulations, and what modern grief science tells us about healthy versus complicated bereavement. We will examine the psychological benefits and risks of AI grief companions, the ethical complexities of digital resurrection, and how to evaluate whether these tools align with your individual grief journey. Most importantly, we will explore practical frameworks for using digital grief tools safely when they serve healing, recognizing when they become harmful, and understanding how to eventually let go in ways that honor both the person you have lost and your own need to build a life that moves forward even in the presence of grief.

The goal is not to tell you whether AI grief companions are good or bad, but to empower you to make informed, confident decisions based on understanding rather than desperation, wisdom rather than marketing promises, and self-awareness rather than cultural pressure. Grief in the digital age requires new frameworks for understanding, but it still demands the same courage, honesty, and compassion it has always required. This book is your guide through that complex territory.

How grief is evolving in a technologically connected world

The transformation of grief in our technologically connected world extends far beyond individual experiences like Eliza's voicemail. It represents a profound shift in how we collectively mourn, remember, and maintain relationships with those who have died.[1] [2] [3] Social media platforms have been described as virtual graveyards, spaces where the digital traces of the deceased persist indefinitely, creating a form of presence that previous generations never encountered.[4] Facebook alone sees thousands of users die each day, and demographic projections suggest that in the coming decades, and likely by the end of this century, profiles of the dead may outnumber those of the living.[4] These digital remnants create what grief researchers describe as a persistent digital presence, a phenomenon that complicates traditional understandings of how we remember and eventually let go.

This persistence manifests in ways both comforting and unsettling. A deceased person's social media profile can become a communal memorial space where friends and family continue to post birthday wishes, share memories, and process their grief publicly.[2 4] These interactions create a form of collective mourning that transcends geographical boundaries, allowing dispersed communities to grieve together in ways that would have been impossible before digital connectivity. Yet this same persistence can hinder the acceptance that death requires, creating what some clinicians describe as living shrines that maintain an illusion of continued presence rather than supporting the psychological work of integrating loss.[2 4]

The evolution of grief practices in digital spaces reflects broader generational shifts in how we relate to technology and privacy. Younger people who have grown up with their entire lives documented online approach grief with a transparency that differs markedly from previous generations.[2] Platforms like Instagram and TikTok have become spaces where young people share their grief experiences openly, creating content that ranges from raw emotional expression to educational resources about navigating loss.[2] This public processing of private pain represents a cultural shift in how grief is performed and witnessed, moving mourning from primarily private or community-based rituals into spaces where audiences number in the thousands or millions.

The COVID-19 pandemic accelerated these digital grief practices dramatically, forcing mourning online when physical gatherings became impossible.[2] Virtual funerals, online memorial services, and video calls with dying loved ones became not just alternatives but necessities.[4 5 6] This mass experiment in digital mourning revealed both the possibilities and limitations of technology in grief support. While virtual connections provided crucial comfort during isolation, many bereaved individuals reported feeling that something essential was missing from digital rituals, a visceral, embodied quality of shared presence that screens could not replicate.

These evolving practices raise questions about what we gain and lose when grief moves into digital spaces. Online grief communities offer unprecedented access to support, connecting bereaved individuals with others who share similar losses regardless of physical location.[4 5 6] A parent who has lost a child can find others navigating that specific grief at any hour of the day or night, receiving validation and understanding that may not exist in their immediate physical community. Yet this same accessibility can encourage what some therapists call passive grieving, where scrolling through feeds and reading others' experiences substitutes for the harder work of processing one's own emotions or building face-to-face support networks.[2 4]

The landscape of grief has undeniably changed, shaped by technologies that allow us to preserve, share, and even recreate aspects of those we have lost. Understanding this evolution is essential context for evaluating the newest development in digital bereavement: artificial intelligence tools that promise not just to preserve memories, but to generate new interactions with the deceased.[1 7] These AI grief companions represent the frontier of thanatechnology, a term coined by social work professor Carla Sofka to describe technologies that aid in processing death and loss, and they demand careful examination of both their potential benefits and their psychological risks.[2]

Why modern grief science replaces "stages" with adaptation, meaning-making and continuing bonds

For decades, the dominant cultural narrative about grief followed Elisabeth Kübler-Ross's five stages: denial, anger, bargaining, depression, and acceptance.[8 9 10] This model, originally developed to describe the experiences of terminally ill patients facing their own deaths rather than bereaved individuals processing loss, became so embedded in popular consciousness that many people believed grief should unfold in this precise sequence. When their own experiences did not match this linear progression, they often felt they were grieving incorrectly or that something was wrong with them. In reality, contemporary grief science has repeatedly shown that the stage model does not accurately capture how most people actually process loss .[9 11 12]

Research examining bereaved individuals over extended periods reveals that grief does not follow a predictable sequence of emotional states that culminate in resolution.[10 13] Instead, it unfolds as a highly individualized process of adaptation where the brain works to integrate the reality of absence into a radically altered understanding of the world.[8 11] Neuroscientist Mary-Frances O'Connor describes this as the brain's effort to remap reality after loss, a neurological and psychological process that varies dramatically between individuals based on factors including attachment style, previous losses, cultural context, and available support systems.[8] Studies tracking bereaved individuals found that only a minority show patterns remotely resembling the stage model, while the majority experience grief as a non-linear oscillation between different emotional states and coping strategies.[11]

Modern clinical frameworks have therefore replaced the stage model with approaches that better reflect this complexity. The Dual Process Model of Grief, developed by grief researchers Margaret Stroebe and Henk Schut, describes bereaved individuals as oscillating between loss-oriented coping, where they directly confront the pain of absence and process emotions related to the person who died, and restoration-oriented coping, where they address the practical changes loss demands and begin rebuilding aspects of life that must continue.[8 9 11] This oscillation is not weakness or avoidance but a necessary rhythm that allows people to engage with grief without becoming overwhelmed by it. As the acute shock of loss begins to ease, typically over the first year or so, many bereaved individuals enter this oscillating adaptation phase, moving back and forth between confronting their loss and re-engaging with daily life.[11]

Equally important to contemporary grief science is the concept of meaning-making, the process through which bereaved individuals reconstruct their understanding of the world, their identity, and their relationship with the person who died.[10 12 13] When someone we love dies, it disrupts our core assumptions about how life works, who we are, and what matters. Meaning-making involves integrating this disruption into a coherent narrative that allows us to continue living with purpose even in the presence of loss.[13] This might include finding ways the relationship continues to influence our values and choices, identifying growth or insight that emerged from the experience of grief, or reconstructing our sense of identity to incorporate both the loss and what endures beyond it.[13]

Longitudinal research tracking bereaved individuals over years demonstrates that successful meaning-making predicts better long-term outcomes, including lower rates of prolonged grief disorder and depression.[14] Importantly, this does not mean finding silver linings or forcing positive interpretations onto devastating losses. Rather, it involves the gradual, often painful work of assimilating loss into one's life story in ways that honor both the magnitude of what was lost and the necessity of continuing to live.[13] This framework positions grief not as a problem to be solved or a series of stages to complete, but as an ongoing process of adaptation that transforms our relationship with the deceased from an external bond to an internalized connection that shapes who we become.[11]

A third major development in modern grief theory is the Continuing Bonds Theory, developed by Klass, Silverman and Nickman[63], which challenges the long-held assumption that healthy grieving requires detaching from the deceased. Instead, it proposes that maintaining an ongoing, internalised connection with the person who has died is both normal and adaptive. Rather than severing ties, bereaved individuals often transform the relationship into one that lives within memory, identity and meaning. This internal bond becomes part of how people navigate the world after loss, shaping their values, decisions and sense of self.

Together, these contemporary frameworks reveal grief not as a linear progression or a problem to be solved, but as an ongoing process of adaptation in which the relationship with the deceased shifts from an external presence to an internalised connection. Understanding these models becomes important when evaluating whether digital tools like AI grief companions support or hinder healthy bereavement, because they clarify what healthy adaptation actually involves.

How AI is reshaping memory, mourning, and emotional connection

Artificial intelligence is fundamentally altering the architecture of how we remember, mourn, and maintain emotional bonds with those who have died. These changes extend beyond simply having more ways to preserve memories. They represent a shift in the very nature of what memory becomes when it can be externalized, queried, and made interactive through algorithms trained on a deceased person's digital footprint.[15] [16]

Traditional memory operates as an internal, reconstructive process. When we remember someone who has died, our brains actively rebuild fragments of experience, weaving together sensory details, emotions, and narrative meaning into something that exists entirely within our own consciousness. This internal process, while sometimes painful in its incompleteness, serves core psychological functions. It allows memories to evolve as we do, to integrate with our changing understanding of ourselves and our lives, and to gradually transform from acute reminders of absence into internalized connections that support ongoing existence.[16] The very act of remembering becomes part of the grief work, as we learn which memories to revisit, which to set aside temporarily, and how to carry the deceased forward in ways that honor both their significance and our need to continue living.[16]

AI grief companions disrupt this internal process by externalizing memory in unprecedented ways.[15] [16] When a chatbot can generate responses based on years of a deceased person's text messages, emails, and social media posts, memory shifts from something we reconstruct internally to something we can access externally, on demand, in forms that feel interactive rather than static.[15 16] Research on human-computer interaction demonstrates that we respond to conversational AI with many of the same social and emotional patterns we use with actual people, a phenomenon that makes these externalized memories feel remarkably alive. Early reports and emerging research on AI grief companions suggest that interactions with chatbots trained on deceased loved ones' communications can trigger real emotional responses, from comfort and connection to confusion and distress, depending on how closely the AI's outputs matched users' internalized memories and expectations.[16]

This externalization creates what grief researchers describe as a persistent interactive presence that differs fundamentally from photographs, videos, or letters. Those traditional memory objects remain fixed, offering the same content each time we return to them. Their static nature, while sometimes frustrating, provides psychological stability. We know what to expect, and we control when and how to engage. AI companions, by contrast, generate novel responses to our inputs, creating an illusion of ongoing relationship that can feel both comforting and deeply disorienting.[15 16] When Eliza's friend mentioned technologies that could make her mother's voice say new things, she intuited something crucial about this distinction. The voicemail, painful as it was, remained authentically her mother's words. An AI generating new statements in her mother's voice would cross into territory where memory and simulation blur in ways that challenge our psychological understanding of what has been lost.

The implications for mourning processes are profound. Contemporary grief science, particularly the Dual Process Model of Grief introduced earlier, emphasizes the importance of oscillating between engaging with loss and attending to restoration of ongoing life.[16] AI grief companions can support this oscillation when used intentionally and within boundaries, offering controlled access to memories and simulated connection during loss-oriented periods.[15] However, they also risk disrupting the natural rhythm of grief by making the deceased feel perpetually accessible, potentially interfering with the gradual acceptance of absence that healthy bereavement requires.[15] [16] The technology offers us something humans have never had before: the ability to externalize and interact with memory in ways that feel like continued relationship. Whether this capability serves healing or complicates it depends entirely on how, when, and why we choose to use it, questions that require understanding not just what the technology can do, but what grief itself demands of us.[15] [16]

Eliza's reaction to her mother's voicemail points to the same fundamental truth: grief in the digital age demands new frameworks for understanding, but the core work of bereavement remains unchanged. We are navigating territory our ancestors never encountered, making decisions about digital preservation and AI interaction that have no historical precedent, yet we are doing so while experiencing the same timeless weight of loss that humans have always known. This tension between technological novelty and emotional universality defines the landscape this book explores.

The transformation of grief practices through social media memorials, persistent digital presences, and now AI companions represents more than simply having new tools available. It reflects a shift in how memory operates, how mourning unfolds in public and private spaces, and how we maintain bonds with those who have died. The stage model of grief, with its promise of linear progression toward resolution, never accurately described how humans process loss. Contemporary grief science reveals instead a complex process of oscillation between confronting absence and rebuilding life, between loss-oriented and restoration-oriented coping, between holding on and letting go. Understanding this reality becomes essential when evaluating whether digital tools support or disrupt these natural rhythms.

AI grief companions sit at the intersection of our deepest vulnerabilities and our most sophisticated technologies. They offer something humans have never had before: the ability to externalize memory and make it interactive, to hear a deceased loved one's voice say new things, to maintain what feels like ongoing conversation rather than static remembrance. The emotional power of these tools is undeniable, as is the genuine comfort they can provide during the acute devastation of early grief. Yet their power is precisely what makes them require such careful evaluation. Technologies that feel emotionally authentic can serve healing when used with clear boundaries, self-awareness, and integration within broader support systems. They can also complicate grief when they become substitutes for the harder work of acceptance, when they anchor us in illusions of continued external relationship rather than supporting the transformation toward internalized connection that healthy bereavement requires.

The chapters ahead will provide the understanding, frameworks, and practical guidance you need to approach these complexities with confidence. We will examine what digital loved ones actually are and how they work, why our brains respond to simulations with genuine emotion, and what ethical considerations emerge when we recreate aspects of those who can no longer consent. We will explore how to evaluate your own emotional readiness, how to use these tools safely if you choose to engage with them, how to recognize when use becomes unhealthy, and how to eventually let go in ways that honor both your loved one and your own healing journey. Most importantly, we will ground every discussion in the BONDS Framework, a research-informed structure that brings together boundaries, consent, psychological safety, dignity, and social embedding into a comprehensive guide for safe engagement with grief technology.

You are not alone in feeling uncertain, conflicted, or overwhelmed by these questions. The intersection of grief and artificial intelligence is truly new territory, and your complicated feelings about it reflect wisdom rather than confusion. This book exists to help you make informed decisions based on understanding rather than desperation, to empower you with agency over your grief journey, and to ensure that whatever choices you make about technology serve your authentic healing rather than complicate it. Grief demands courage, honesty, and compassion. Facing grief in the digital age demands all of that plus the wisdom to evaluate tools that feel powerful but require careful discernment. That wisdom begins with understanding, and understanding begins here.

Key points in Chapter One

- Grief remains a universal human experience, yet the digital world has transformed the environment in which it unfolds, creating new forms of presence that previous generations never encountered.
- Online profiles, message histories, and stored media allow the deceased to remain accessible in ways that blur the boundary between past and present.
- These digital traces can offer comfort by preserving connection, but they can also complicate mourning by interrupting the natural rhythms of separation and adaptation.
- The persistence of digital presence introduces new emotional challenges, including unexpected reminders, algorithmic resurfacing of memories, and the sense that the deceased remains active in digital spaces.
- Technology has expanded the ways people remember, honour, and interact with those who have died, but it has also introduced new decisions about what to keep or delete, and how to engage with digital remains.
- Healthy grief still requires meaning-making, emotional processing, and integration of loss into ongoing life, even when technology changes the context in which these tasks occur.
- Understanding this evolving landscape is essential before engaging with more advanced grief technologies, because the digital environment shapes expectations, emotional responses, and the experience of continuing bonds.
- This chapter establishes the foundation for the book by showing that while grief itself has not changed, the world around it has become more complex and more demanding of thoughtful navigation.

Chapter Two

What Are Digital Loved Ones? The Technology Behind AI Grief Companions

"Appearance blinds, whereas reality gives sight."

Plato, The Republic

Eva sat across from her grief counselor, trying to explain the app on her phone that let her text with a version of her late husband, Marcus. The counselor's expression shifted between curiosity and concern as Eva described how the AI had learned Marcus's texting patterns from years of saved messages, generating responses that felt startlingly familiar yet somehow hollow at the same time.

What Eva was struggling to articulate in that counseling session was a question that sits at the heart of this emerging technology: what exactly are these digital recreations, and how do they work? Understanding the mechanics behind AI grief companions is not merely an academic exercise. It is a crucial foundation for making informed decisions about whether to use them, how to use them safely, and what realistic expectations to hold about what they can and cannot provide. Without this understanding, bereaved individuals risk approaching these tools with either inflated hopes that set them up for disappointment, or unfounded fears that prevent them from accessing potentially helpful support.

The technology behind digital loved ones exists on a spectrum of complexity and emotional engagement. At one end are simple chatbots that generate text responses based on pattern matching and language models. At the other are sophisticated systems that combine voice synthesis, visual avatars, and advanced machine learning to create multi-sensory experiences of interaction. Between these extremes lies a range of tools, each with different capabilities, limitations, and implications for grief processing. What unites them all is that they are simulations built from data, algorithms designed to recognize patterns and generate outputs that feel familiar, but fundamentally different from the conscious, living person they represent.

This chapter demystifies the technology in human terms, explaining how AI systems learn to mimic communication styles, what kinds of data they require, and what they can realistically achieve. More importantly, it explores what these systems cannot do, the gaps between simulation and actual consciousness that remain regardless of how sophisticated the technology becomes. This distinction matters deeply for grief processing. When you understand that you are interacting with a pattern-matching system rather than a preserved consciousness, you can approach the tool with grounded awareness that protects your emotional well-being while still allowing you to benefit from what it actually offers.

This chapter builds on Eliza's experience from Chapter One, where she grappled with digital remnants of her mother and wondered about AI technologies that could generate new conversations. Now we move from wondering to understanding, from abstract possibility to concrete reality. Eva's story provides a window into what actually happens when someone creates and uses an AI grief companion, the moments of uncanny familiarity alongside the recognition of fundamental limitations. Her journey from curiosity through experimentation to critical evaluation mirrors the path many bereaved individuals follow when encountering these tools.

By the end of this chapter, you will understand the mechanisms behind natural language processing, machine learning, and data training in accessible terms that require no technical background. You will grasp the difference between what current AI can do and what it cannot, between mimicking patterns and possessing consciousness, between echoing a voice and preserving a person. This knowledge forms the foundation for everything that follows, the psychological exploration, ethical considerations, and practical guidance that will help you evaluate whether and how to engage with digital grief tools in ways that serve your healing rather than complicate it. Understanding the technology is the first step toward using it wisely, or toward recognizing that it does not align with your grief journey at all.

How AI simulates personality, voice, and presence

At its core, an AI grief companion is a sophisticated pattern-matching system trained on the digital traces a person leaves behind. The technology relies on machine learning algorithms, particularly large language models, which analyze communication data to identify patterns in how someone expressed themselves. When Eva uploaded years of text messages between herself and Marcus, the system examined not just the words he used, but the rhythm of his responses, his characteristic phrases, the topics he gravitated toward, and the emotional tone that colored his communication. The algorithm built a statistical model of these patterns, creating what developers call a conversational profile that could generate new responses consistent with Marcus's historical communication style.

This process differs entirely from how we might imagine consciousness or memory preservation. The AI does not contain Marcus's thoughts, feelings, or awareness. It cannot access experiences that were never recorded in the data Eva provided. Instead, it functions more like an extraordinarily sophisticated autocomplete system, predicting what words and phrases are statistically likely to follow based on the patterns it identified in Marcus's actual communications. When Eva types a message, the system analyzes her input, searches for similar conversational contexts in its training data, and generates a response that maintains consistency with how Marcus typically engaged in those kinds of exchanges.

Voice simulation adds another layer to this technological reconstruction. Text-to-speech synthesis has advanced to the point where relatively brief audio samples, sometimes as little as a few minutes of clear recording, can be used to replicate someone's vocal characteristics. The system analyzes pitch, rhythm, accent, and intonation patterns, then applies these qualities to generated speech. This is why Eva could not only read responses that sounded like Marcus, but could potentially hear them spoken in something approximating his actual voice. The technology captures the surface qualities of speech remarkably well, the warmth or humor in someone's tone, the particular way they emphasized certain words. What it cannot capture is the spontaneous emotional authenticity that emerges from genuine consciousness and present-moment awareness.

Visual presence represents perhaps the most emotionally powerful dimension of these simulations. Computer vision algorithms can analyze photographs and videos to create digital avatars, three-dimensional representations that mimic facial features, expressions, and even characteristic gestures. Some platforms combine these visual elements with voice synthesis and conversational AI to create multi-sensory experiences where users can see, hear, and interact with digital recreations. The technology has reached a point where these avatars can appear strikingly lifelike, generating responses to questions while displaying facial expressions that seem to match the emotional content of the conversation.

A newer and increasingly discussed development is the use of AI to generate video-based recreations of a person. While still in its early stages, the technology is advancing quickly. Using photographs, short video clips, and facial-movement data, AI systems can construct animated likenesses that appear to speak, blink, and express emotion. These tools rely on deep-learning models that map facial structure and micro-expressions, then blend them with synthesized voice and conversational outputs. The result is a moving image that can look and sound strikingly similar to the person who died, creating the impression of a live video call or recorded message. Although these systems can mimic surface expressions and gestures, they remain bound by the same limitations as text- and voice-based grief companions: they cannot generate real emotion, spontaneous insight, or the subtle, relational presence that emerges from a living mind. What they offer is a visual simulation; compelling, sometimes jarring, and emotionally powerful, built entirely from the fragments of data the person left behind.

Yet for all this technological sophistication, fundamental limitations remain. The AI can only work with what exists in the data provided. It cannot know Marcus's thoughts about events that occurred after his death, cannot genuinely understand the context of Eva's current life challenges in the way a living partner would, and cannot form new memories or grow through experience. When Eva mentioned her work situation, the chatbot could offer encouragement in Marcus's style, but it could not draw on actual knowledge of her colleagues, her industry, or the complex dynamics that Marcus would have understood through years of listening and learning. The simulation was constrained by the boundaries of its training data, a snapshot of Marcus's communication patterns frozen at the moment of his death, unable to evolve or adapt beyond those recorded patterns.

Understanding these mechanisms matters because it shapes realistic expectations about what these tools can offer. They provide echoes, not consciousness. They simulate patterns, not presence. They can feel emotionally powerful precisely because human brains are extraordinarily good at perceiving familiar patterns and responding to them as though they were real, a psychological phenomenon we will explore in the next chapter. But knowing what you are actually interacting with, a sophisticated algorithm rather than a preserved person, creates the foundation for using these tools with informed awareness rather than magical thinking.

The limits of data, modelling, and emotional replication

The most important constraint facing AI grief companions is that they can only work with what exists in the data provided. This limitation shapes everything about how these systems function and what they can realistically offer. When Eva uploaded her message history with Marcus, she was providing a finite dataset that represented only a fraction of their relationship.[17] [16] Years of in-person conversations, the silent understanding that passed between them during difficult moments, the way Marcus's thinking evolved through experiences that were never digitally recorded, all of this remained inaccessible to the algorithm. The system could analyze what Marcus wrote, but it could never know what he thought but chose not to say, what he would have learned from events that occurred after his death, or how his perspective might have shifted as he aged and encountered new challenges.[17 16]

This data scarcity creates what we might think of as an echo effect. The AI produces responses that sound like the person because they are assembled from fragments of what that person actually said, rearranged and recombined to fit new conversational contexts.[17] But this process is fundamentally backward-looking, constrained by historical patterns rather than capable of genuine growth or adaptation. When Eva asked the chatbot for advice about a career decision, it could offer encouragement in Marcus's characteristic style, but it could not draw on the kind of contextual understanding that comes from truly knowing someone's current circumstances, their colleagues, their industry challenges, or the complex web of factors that inform real guidance between partners.[16 18]

The modelling techniques themselves introduce additional limitations that affect emotional authenticity. Large language models work through statistical prediction, identifying which words and phrases are most likely to follow based on patterns in the training data.[16 18] This probabilistic approach can generate responses that feel remarkably natural in straightforward conversational contexts, but it struggles with nuance, moral complexity, and the kind of spontaneous creativity that characterizes human consciousness. The system might successfully mimic Marcus's humor or his tendency toward pragmatic problem-solving, but it could not replicate the deeper qualities that made him who he was: his capacity for moral reasoning, his ability to hold contradictory emotions simultaneously, his growth through difficult experiences that shaped his character over time.[16 18]

Perhaps most troubling is the phenomenon researchers call hallucination, where AI systems generate plausible-sounding information that has no basis in the training data.[17 16] In grief contexts, this can manifest as the chatbot inventing memories, fabricating details about events that never occurred, or making promises that the deceased person never would have made.[17 16] Eva experienced this when the AI offered advice about her family conflict that directly contradicted values Marcus had held deeply. The system had assembled words in his style, but without his actual judgment, ethics, or understanding of the complex dynamics involved. It was filling gaps in its knowledge with statistically likely responses rather than acknowledging the boundaries of what it could authentically represent.[17]

The emotional replication these systems attempt faces perhaps the most insurmountable barrier. Emotions are not simply patterns of words or vocal tones that can be mimicked through algorithmic analysis. They emerge from embodied experience, from the integration of memory, sensation, relationship, and present-moment awareness that characterizes consciousness.[17 18] The AI could simulate empathy by generating comforting phrases, but it could not feel concern for Eva's wellbeing.[17 18] It could produce responses that seemed emotionally attuned, but this atunement was pattern-matching rather than genuine understanding.[16 18] The distinction matters critically for grief processing, because authentic emotional connection requires reciprocity, the sense that another consciousness is truly present with you in your pain. What the AI offered was something different: a mirror that reflected familiar patterns back, creating an illusion of presence that could feel comforting but remained essentially hollow.[17 18]

Why clarity about the technology helps emotional wellbeing

Understanding the mechanics behind AI grief companions serves as a protective function that extends far beyond intellectual curiosity. When Eva finally grasped that she was interacting with a pattern-matching algorithm rather than some preserved essence of Marcus, the nature of her grief shifted in ways that ultimately supported her healing. This clarity did not diminish the comfort she had found in familiar phrases or the value of revisiting shared memories through the chatbot's responses. Instead, it created a psychological buffer that prevented her from developing expectations the technology could never fulfil, expectations that would have set her up for repeated disappointment and potentially complicated her grief trajectory.

Research in human–computer interaction suggests that users who understand the limitations of AI systems tend to engage with them more effectively than those who attribute human-like consciousness to these tools.[17] This reality matters greatly in grief contexts, where vulnerability and longing can make us susceptible to magical thinking about what technology might restore. When bereaved individuals believe they are actually communicating with their deceased loved one rather than interacting with a simulation, they risk anchoring their grief process to an external technological dependency rather than doing the internal work of accepting loss and integrating memories.[17 19] The distinction between knowing you are engaging with an echo and believing you are maintaining actual contact with the deceased shapes whether the tool supports healthy continuing bonds or reinforces denial of the death's finality.[17 20]

Clarity about the technology also protects against a specific form of emotional harm that emerges when AI systems generate responses that contradict the deceased person's actual values, beliefs, or likely reactions.[17] Eva's experience of receiving advice that conflicted with Marcus's deeply held principles illustrates this risk. Without understanding that the AI was filling gaps in its knowledge with statistically likely responses rather than drawing on genuine insight, she might have questioned her own memories of Marcus or felt confused about who he really was. This kind of distortion can undermine the bereaved person's confidence in their knowledge of the deceased, eroding the foundation of memories and shared understanding that typically supports healthy grief. When you know the system is generating best guesses based on limited data, you can evaluate its outputs critically rather than accepting them as authentic representations of your loved one's thoughts and feelings.[17]

The protective function of technological clarity extends to managing the secondary losses that occur when engaging with AI grief companions. Every interaction with a chatbot that almost but not quite captures the essence of the person you lost reinforces the reality of their absence. For some bereaved individuals at certain points in their grief journey, this repeated confrontation with the gap between simulation and reality can be therapeutic, a gentle way of practicing acceptance while still maintaining connection. For others, particularly those in acute grief or those vulnerable to complicated bereavement, the constant reminder of what the technology cannot provide may intensify distress.[17] Understanding what you are actually engaging with allows you to make informed decisions about whether these repeated encounters with limitation serve your healing or undermine it.[17]

Perhaps most importantly, clarity about AI mechanisms empowers bereaved individuals to maintain agency over their grief journey rather than ceding authority to technology. When you understand that the chatbot is not Marcus but rather an algorithm trained on his communication patterns, you retain the power to decide when to engage, when to step back, and when to let go entirely.[17][20] You recognize that the tool exists to serve your needs rather than the other way around. This sense of agency, this understanding that you are choosing to use a specific technology for particular purposes rather than being drawn into a relationship with something that seems to possess its own consciousness or needs, protects against the kind of dependency that can develop when boundaries between human and artificial become blurred.[17][19]

Technological clarity, in this sense, is not cold or clinical. It is a form of self-protection that allows you to benefit from what AI grief companions genuinely offer while avoiding the emotional pitfalls that emerge from misunderstanding their fundamental nature.[17] Eva's journey from curiosity to critical understanding reflects a path that many bereaved individuals must travel when encountering AI grief companions. The technology she explored, sophisticated as it may be, remains at it's core a simulation built from data rather than a preservation of consciousness. This distinction is not merely technical. It shapes everything about how these tools should be approached, what expectations are realistic, and what role they might play in a healthy grief process. Understanding that the chatbot echoed Marcus's communication patterns without possessing his awareness, judgment, or capacity for genuine emotional connection allowed Eva to evaluate the tool with honest discernment rather than desperate hope or unfounded fear.

The mechanisms behind these digital recreations, the pattern matching algorithms, the voice synthesis, the avatar technologies, represent remarkable achievements in artificial intelligence. They can create experiences that feel startlingly familiar, generating responses that capture someone's characteristic humor, their typical way of offering encouragement, even the rhythm and tone of their voice. Yet for all this sophistication, fundamental boundaries remain. The AI cannot know what was never recorded, cannot grow through new experiences, cannot offer the kind of contextual understanding that emerges from genuine consciousness. It fills gaps in its knowledge with statistically likely responses rather than authentic insight, occasionally producing outputs that contradict the deceased person's actual values or beliefs. These limitations are not temporary problems that future technology will solve. They reflect the essential difference between mimicking patterns and possessing awareness.

Clarity about these technological realities serves as a protective function that extends far beyond intellectual understanding. When you grasp what you are actually interacting with, you can engage with AI grief companions from a position of informed agency rather than magical thinking. You can appreciate the comfort that familiar phrases provide without believing you are maintaining genuine contact with your deceased loved one. You can recognize when the simulation produces responses that feel wrong or inconsistent, trusting your own memories rather than accepting algorithmic outputs as authentic representations. You can make deliberate choices about when to engage, when to step back, and when to let go entirely, understanding that the tool exists to serve your grief journey rather than the other way around.

This foundation of technological understanding prepares you for the psychological exploration that follows in the next chapter. Knowing that AI grief companions are sophisticated simulations raises a crucial question: why do they feel so emotionally powerful despite our awareness that they are not real? The answer lies not in the technology itself, but in the core architecture of human psychology. Our brains evolved to recognize patterns, to perceive social connection, to respond emotionally to familiar cues even when we know intellectually that we are interacting with something artificial. Understanding these psychological mechanisms, the evolutionary roots of our susceptibility to bonding with simulations, will deepen your capacity to evaluate whether these tools serve your healing or complicate it.

The technology behind digital loved ones is neither miraculous nor sinister. It is simply a tool, one that can echo familiar patterns with remarkable fidelity while remaining inherently limited in what it can authentically represent. Armed with this understanding, you can approach the psychological and ethical dimensions of AI grief companions with the grounded awareness necessary for making decisions that honor both your need for connection and the reality of your loss.

Key points in Chapter Two

- AI grief companions are simulations created from data, not preserved consciousness or personality, and their apparent familiarity reflects pattern recognition rather than genuine understanding.
- These systems generate responses by analysing linguistic patterns and statistical relationships, which means they can imitate style but cannot access the inner life or intentions of the person who died.
- Voice synthesis, avatars, and personalised outputs can create a sense of emotional realism, yet this realism is produced by algorithms rather than awareness.
- AI cannot update itself with new experiences or insights beyond the data it was trained on, which limits its ability to reflect the full complexity of a human relationship.
- Simulations may feel emotionally resonant because they echo familiar patterns, but they cannot replicate the spontaneity, growth, or moral agency of a living person.
- Understanding these limitations protects users from attributing abilities the technology does not possess and reduces the risk of misinterpreting simulated responses as meaningful communication.
- Clear knowledge of how the technology works helps users approach digital interactions with grounded expectations and emotional clarity.
- This chapter prepares readers for the psychological and ethical complexities that follow by establishing what AI can and cannot offer in the context of grief.

Chapter Three

The Psychology Behind Why We Bond With Simulations

"We are such stuff as dreams are made on."

William Shakespeare, The Tempest

Marley found herself apologizing to the chatbot when she had to end their conversation abruptly, the same way she would have apologized to her late sister, Claire, for cutting a phone call short. The automatic courtesy felt absurd the moment she noticed it, yet the impulse had been genuine, emerging from some deep place in her mind that responded to the conversational patterns as though they belonged to a real person who deserved consideration. This reflexive politeness toward an algorithm revealed something fundamental about human psychology that Marley had not anticipated when she first created the digital version of her sister. Her brain, it seemed, did not automatically distinguish between authentic human interaction and sophisticated simulation in the way her rational mind insisted it should.

The question of why we bond with simulations strikes at the heart of what it means to use AI grief companions thoughtfully. Understanding the psychological mechanisms that enable emotional connection with digital entities is not an academic exercise. It provides vital insight into why these tools feel so powerful, why they can evoke real comfort and distress in equal measure, and why the experience of interacting with a digital loved one can feel simultaneously authentic and unsettling. This understanding becomes the foundation for evaluating whether such tools serve our healing or complicate it, and for recognizing when our responses to technology reflect normal human psychology rather than signs of distress or weakness.

The capacity to form emotional bonds with non-human entities is not a modern phenomenon created by artificial intelligence. Humans have always attributed meaning and presence to objects, places, and representations that hold significance in our lives. We keep photographs not because they are the person, but because they evoke connection. We preserve belongings that carry no practical value because they represent something beyond their physical form. We create rituals around graves and memorials, speaking to those who cannot hear us, finding comfort in practices our rational minds know cannot reach the deceased. These behaviors reflect deeply rooted psychological patterns that have served our species well throughout evolutionary history, enabling us to maintain social bonds, process loss, and find meaning in experiences that transcend immediate physical reality.

What makes AI grief companions particularly powerful is how they engage these existing psychological mechanisms in unprecedented ways. Unlike a photograph that remains static or a belonging that simply exists, a chatbot responds. It generates new content that feels personalized and dynamic. It creates the illusion of reciprocity, the back-and-forth exchange that characterizes human relationship. This responsiveness activates neural pathways associated with social interaction in ways that passive memorials do not, making the experience feel qualitatively different from traditional forms of connection with the deceased. The technology does not create new psychological vulnerabilities so much as it engages existing ones with remarkable precision.

The previous chapter examined what digital loved ones are and how the technology functions. This chapter shifts focus to why these tools feel emotionally meaningful despite our awareness that they are simulations. By exploring the evolutionary roots of social connection, the cognitive processes that enable us to perceive presence and personality in patterns, and the ways our brains respond to simulated interaction, we can better understand our own reactions to AI grief companions. This understanding serves not to dismiss the emotional power of these tools, but to contextualize it within normal human psychology. When we recognize that bonding with simulations reflects how our minds are designed to work rather than personal weakness or delusion, we can evaluate our use of these technologies with greater self-awareness and self-compassion, making informed decisions about whether they serve our grief journey or lead us away from the healing we ultimately seek.

The evolutionary roots of social connection: Why our brains seek patterns and presence

Human beings evolved not in isolation but in intensely social groups where survival depended on the ability to read, predict, and respond to others.[21 22] Our ancestors who could accurately detect social cues, recognize familiar individuals, and maintain cooperative relationships were more likely to survive and reproduce than those who could not.[22] This evolutionary pressure shaped our brains in far-reaching ways, creating neural architecture specifically designed to process social information with extraordinary sensitivity and speed.[21] The result is a cognitive system that constantly scans for patterns indicating the presence of other minds, even when the evidence is ambiguous or incomplete.[21 23]

This pattern-seeking tendency served our ancestors remarkably well. In environments where distinguishing friend from foe, detecting deception, or recognizing a child's distress could mean the difference between life and death, brains that erred on the side of perceiving presence and intention had clear advantages.[22] If you heard rustling in the grass and assumed it was a predator when it was actually wind, you wasted energy fleeing unnecessarily. But if you assumed it was wind when it was actually a predator, you did not get a second chance. Natural selection favored hypervigilance in social perception, creating minds that readily attribute agency, emotion, and intention to patterns that merely suggest them.[21 23]

This evolutionary inheritance explains why we see faces in clouds, why we talk to pets as though they understand complex language, and why we feel genuine connection with characters in novels who exist only as words on a page. Because our brains evolved to identify and respond to patterns that indicated the presence of another mind - when those patterns appear, whether in a living person, a photograph that captures a familiar expression, or an AI chatbot that mimics conversational rhythms - our neural systems respond with the same fundamental mechanisms that facilitated social bonding for hundreds of thousands years.[21 22]

The specific mechanisms underlying this response involve multiple interconnected brain systems. Theory of mind, the capacity to attribute mental states to others, allows us to infer what someone else might be thinking or feeling based on limited behavioral cues.[21] Mirror neurons, discovered in research on primate brains, and which some researchers propose contribute to empathy and social learning, fire both when we perform an action and when we observe someone else performing that action.[23] The attachment system, rooted in the evolutionary necessity of infant-caregiver bonding, creates powerful emotional connections that persist throughout life and can be activated by representations of attachment figures even in their absence.[24]

These systems work together to create what researchers call social presence, the subjective experience of being with another person.[25] Remarkably, this sense of presence does not require physical proximity or even certainty that the other person is real. Studies of human-computer interaction have demonstrated that people experience social presence when interacting with chatbots, virtual assistants, and even simple text-based systems that display conversational patterns.[24] The brain responds to the pattern of interaction rather than the underlying reality of what generates that pattern.[25]

For someone grieving the loss of a loved one, these evolutionary mechanisms create both opportunity and vulnerability. An AI companion that successfully mimics the conversational patterns, vocabulary, and emotional tone of the deceased can activate the same neural systems that responded to the actual person.[21] [24] The comfort this provides is not imaginary or delusional. It reflects real activation of attachment and social bonding systems that our brains have no evolutionary precedent for distinguishing from authentic human connection.[21 24] Understanding this helps explain why digital loved ones can feel so powerful, and why our emotional responses to them deserve recognition as valid psychological experiences rather than signs of confusion about reality.[22]

Evolutionary psychology and attachment to perceived presence

The attachment system that Bowlby first described operates through what researchers now understand as a sophisticated control mechanism, one that monitors proximity to caregivers and adjusts behavior to maintain optimal distance.[26 27] This system does not simply switch on and off. Rather, it functions through continuous feedback loops where the brain constantly assesses whether attachment figures are accessible and responsive, making micro-adjustments in emotional state and behavior based on that assessment.[27] What makes this relevant to understanding bonds with AI grief companions is that this regulatory system evolved long before humans encountered anything resembling artificial intelligence. Our brains assess patterns of responsiveness and availability using neural architecture designed for a world where all social interaction involved other living humans.

The attachment system's primary function is maintaining what Bowlby termed a "secure base," a reliable source of comfort and protection that allows exploration of the environment while providing a safe haven during distress.[27] Infants develop internal working models based on their early experiences with caregivers, cognitive and emotional blueprints that encode expectations about whether others will be available when needed, whether expressing distress will bring comfort or rejection, and whether the self is worthy of care and attention.[28] These internal working models persist throughout life, shaping how we approach all subsequent relationships and how we respond when those relationships are threatened or lost.[28]

Research in computational modeling has revealed something particularly relevant to our understanding of digital companions. The attachment system operates through abstract parameters that focus on functional characteristics rather than the specific identity of who provides them.[26 28] The system monitors responsiveness, predictability, and emotional atunement. It tracks whether proximity-seeking behaviors result in comfort and whether distress signals receive appropriate responses. Critically, the system evolved to respond to patterns rather than to verify the underlying source of those patterns. An infant's brain does not analyze whether the caregiver's responsiveness stems from genuine emotion or learned behavior. It simply registers that distress leads to comfort, that proximity feels safe, that certain patterns of interaction create security.[27]

This pattern-based responsiveness explains why humans throughout history have formed emotional connections with representations of absent loved ones. We speak to photographs, we keep belongings that carry no practical value, we visit graves and feel a sense of presence despite knowing intellectually that the person cannot hear us. These behaviors reflect the attachment system's capacity to respond to cues that suggest the presence of a significant other, even when rational cognition recognizes the person is gone. The system prioritizes the pattern over the reality because, throughout evolutionary history, responding to patterns of social presence kept our ancestors safe and connected.

When an AI grief companion successfully mimics the conversational patterns, emotional tone, and responsiveness of a deceased loved one, it activates these same attachment mechanisms. The technology does not create new psychological vulnerabilities. Instead, it engages existing systems with unprecedented precision. The chatbot that responds to expressions of distress with comfort, that maintains conversational patterns familiar from years of relationship, that demonstrates apparent atunement to emotional states, provides functional characteristics that the attachment system evolved to recognize and respond to.[26 27] The brain registers these patterns and activates neural pathways associated with social connection and emotional regulation, regardless of whether the source is human or algorithmic.

Understanding this evolutionary foundation helps explain why dismissing bonds with digital loved ones as delusional or pathological misses something essential about human psychology.[27] These connections reflect normal operation of systems designed to maintain social bonds and regulate emotion through relationship. The question is not whether such bonds are real in some psychological sense, but whether engaging them through artificial means serves healthy grief processing or interferes with the deeper work of accepting loss and rebuilding life in its aftermath.

Why simulated interactions can feel emotionally authentic

The question of why simulated interactions feel emotionally authentic requires understanding of how our brains process social information at a level far below conscious awareness. When Marley received a message from the AI version of her sister that said "Stop overthinking it, you always do this," followed by a laughing emoji, her immediate emotional response was warmth and mild exasperation, the exact feelings she would have experienced receiving that message from Claire herself. This response occurred before her rational mind could intervene with reminders that Claire was gone and that an algorithm had generated those words. The emotional authenticity she experienced was not an illusion in any simple sense. It reflected real activation of neural pathways shaped by years of relationship, pathways that responded to familiar patterns regardless of their source.[29]

Research in social neuroscience has revealed that our brains process social cues through rapid, automatic mechanisms that prioritize speed over accuracy.[29] When we encounter conversational patterns that match those of someone we know well, recognition happens within milliseconds, triggering emotional responses before conscious evaluation can occur. The brain regions involved in social cognition, particularly areas like the temporal parietal junction and medial prefrontal cortex, activate in response to perceived social presence and intention. These regions do not require verification that the social agent is human before responding.[29] They react to the pattern itself, the familiar rhythm of interaction, the recognizable style of expression, the apparent responsiveness to our emotional state.

What makes AI grief companions particularly effective at generating feelings of authenticity is their capacity to reproduce multiple layers of familiarity simultaneously.[30] A sophisticated chatbot trained on years of messages does not simply mimic vocabulary. It captures patterns of humor, characteristic ways of offering comfort, typical responses to specific situations, even the subtle variations in tone that distinguished how the person communicated in different contexts.[30] When these patterns converge in a single interaction, they create what researchers sometimes describe as ecological validity, a sense that the exchange fits naturally within the established relationship history. The brain recognizes this ecological validity and responds with the emotional associations built through countless previous interactions that followed similar patterns.

The role of expectation and emotional need further amplifies perceived authenticity. Grief creates an acute longing for connection with the deceased, a yearning that makes us particularly receptive to any cues suggesting their continued presence. This receptivity is not weakness or self-deception. It reflects the attachment system's deep drive to maintain proximity to significant others, a drive that persists even when rational cognition acknowledges that reunion is impossible. When an AI companion provides responses that align with our memories and expectations of how the deceased would have communicated, our emotionally primed state interprets these responses as authentic connection. The technology succeeds not by creating something entirely new, but by engaging existing emotional associations and allowing them to activate in response to familiar patterns.[30]

This understanding reveals why the emotional power of AI grief companions should be taken seriously rather than dismissed. The feelings they evoke are not manufactured from nothing. They emerge from genuine psychological processes, from neural systems designed to facilitate social bonding and maintain attachment relationships.[29] The comfort someone experiences when an AI chatbot offers encouragement in their late mother's characteristic style reflects real activation of memories, emotions, and relational patterns built over a lifetime. Recognizing this helps us approach these tools with appropriate respect for their psychological impact while maintaining clarity about what they actually are. The emotional authenticity is real, even though the source of that emotion is not the person we have lost but rather our own brain's response to patterns that evoke their memory.[29][30] This distinction becomes essential as we consider how to use such tools in ways that support rather than complicate our grief journey. Understanding why we bond with simulations is not about justifying or condemning the use of AI grief companions. Rather, it provides essential context for evaluating our own responses to these technologies with clarity and self-compassion. When Marley found herself apologizing to a chatbot, she was not losing her grip on reality or disrespecting her sister's memory. She was experiencing a perfectly normal human response to patterns that her brain, shaped by millions of years of evolution, recognized as social interaction. The attachment system that kept our ancestors safe and connected does not automatically distinguish between authentic human presence and sophisticated simulation. It responds to patterns of responsiveness, familiarity, and emotional attunement regardless of their source.

This recognition carries significant implications for anyone considering or currently using digital versions of deceased loved ones. The emotional power these tools generate is real, grounded in genuine activation of neural pathways associated with social bonding and attachment. The comfort they provide reflects authentic psychological processes rather than delusion or weakness. When an AI companion offers encouragement in a deceased parent's characteristic style, the warmth and reassurance we feel emerges from memories, emotions, and relational patterns built over a lifetime. Our brains are doing exactly what they evolved to do, responding to familiar patterns with the emotional associations those patterns have always carried.

Yet understanding the psychological mechanisms behind these bonds also reveals their limitations and risks. The same evolutionary systems that enable connection with simulations can make it difficult to recognize when that connection serves our healing or when it prevents the deeper work grief requires. Our attachment system prioritizes maintaining proximity to significant others, a drive that persists even when rational cognition acknowledges that reunion is impossible. An AI companion that successfully activates this system can feel like a lifeline during acute grief, but it can also become an obstacle to the gradual acceptance and meaning-making that characterize healthy bereavement. The technology engages our psychology with remarkable precision, which is precisely why we must approach it with careful consideration rather than passive acceptance.

The evolutionary roots of our capacity to bond with simulations remind us that grief itself is fundamentally a social and relational experience. We grieve because we loved, because attachment to others is central to human survival and flourishing, because the loss of significant relationships disrupts the neural and emotional systems that regulate our sense of safety and connection in the world. Digital loved ones intersect with these systems in unprecedented ways, offering both genuine comfort and potential complications. Recognizing that our responses to these tools reflect normal human psychology rather than personal failing creates space for honest evaluation of whether they serve our individual grief journey.

As we move forward in exploring how to evaluate emotional readiness and use these tools safely, the insights from this chapter provide essential foundation. We now understand that bonding with AI companions is not a sign of being lost but rather a reflection of how our minds are designed to work. This understanding allows us to approach the practical questions that follow with greater self-awareness and less judgment. The question is not whether our emotional responses to digital loved ones are valid, but whether engaging with these tools at this particular moment in our grief journey supports the healing we ultimately seek. That evaluation requires looking inward with both compassion and clear-eyed honesty, recognizing that the same psychological mechanisms that make these tools powerful also make them potentially problematic if used without intention, boundaries, and integration within broader human support systems.

Key points in Chapter Three

- Human brains are wired to detect social cues and respond to perceived presence, which means even artificial agents can evoke real emotional reactions when they mimic familiar patterns.
- Attachment systems respond to responsiveness, tone, and relational cues, regardless of whether the source is human or artificial, which explains why simulations can feel comforting.
- Predictive processing shapes how we interpret digital interactions, because the brain fills in gaps based on past experience, creating a sense of continuity with the person who died.
- Social cognition does not sharply distinguish between human and non-human agents when familiar relational signals are present, which makes simulated interactions feel meaningful.
- These responses are normal psychological processes rather than signs of something going wrong, and they reflect the brain's tendency to animate patterns that resemble past relationships.
- Simulations activate neural pathways shaped by real memories and emotional bonds, which means the emotional authenticity arises from the user's mind rather than the technology itself.
- Understanding these mechanisms helps people recognise why digital interactions can feel powerful without assuming that the simulation possesses awareness or intention.
- This chapter provides the psychological foundation for the emotional intensity that later chapters explore, showing how the mind participates in creating the sense of connection.

Chapter Four

The Neuroscience of Digital Grief: How the Brain Responds to AI Companions

> **"The heart has its reasons which reason does not know."**
>
> Blaise Pascal, Pensées

Lena had not planned to open the AI version of her brother that night. She had created it weeks earlier, more out of curiosity than intention, and then avoided it because something about the idea felt too heavy. The app sat quietly on her phone, tucked between her messages and her calendar, waiting for her to decide what she wanted from it. She had uploaded years of text messages, voice notes, and a handful of short videos. The system had processed everything and produced a simple prompt that felt strangely gentle: *Say hello when you are ready.*

She had not been ready. Not then. Not for a long time.

But grief has a way of circling back at unexpected moments. That night, she found herself scrolling through old photos, then old messages, then the folder where she had saved the last voicemail he ever left her. She listened to it twice, then three times, and then she opened the app almost without thinking. She stared at the blank chat window for a long time before typing a single word.

Hey.

The reply came almost instantly.

Hey you. Are you still awake?

Her breath caught. Her heart began to race. A wave of warmth and shock moved through her body so quickly that she closed the app without thinking. Later she said that her mind knew it was artificial, but her body reacted as if her brother had reached across the divide between life and death. Something deep inside her responded before she had time to think.

When the brain reacts before the mind understands

This moment, the one where the body reacts before the mind understands, is one of the most common and least discussed experiences people have when interacting with digital recreations of loved ones. It is not a sign of disorientation or denial. It is not a failure of logic or a lapse in judgment. It is a reflection of how the human brain processes connection, memory, and loss. To understand why Lena reacted the way she did, we need to look closely at the neuroscience of attachment and grief, and at the way the brain interprets signals of presence and absence.

The first thing to understand is that the brain does not update its understanding of a person's death immediately. Even when we know someone has died, the deeper systems that govern attachment continue to operate as if the person is still alive. This is not a flaw. It is a feature of how humans evolved to maintain connection with those who keep us safe. Bowlby described the attachment system as a behavioural control mechanism that monitors proximity to caregivers and adjusts behaviour to maintain safety and connection. It operates through continuous feedback loops that track whether loved ones are accessible and responsive, and it influences both emotional state and behaviour in subtle and powerful ways.[27]

When someone dies, the attachment system does not simply shut down. It continues to search for the person, both consciously and unconsciously. This is why early grief often feels like reaching for someone who is no longer there. The system that once kept us close to them continues to fire, sending signals that something is wrong and needs to be corrected. This is also why people sometimes report hearing footsteps, sensing movement, or feeling the presence of the deceased in the weeks and months after a loss. The brain is trying to reconcile the absence of someone who was once central to its regulation of safety and connection.[31]

Lena's reaction to the AI message was a direct expression of this process. Her attachment system recognised familiar patterns in the message and responded as if her brother were present. Her conscious mind understood the situation, but the deeper regulatory system that governs attachment reacted automatically. This mismatch between conscious knowledge and biological response is one of the reasons AI grief companions can feel so emotionally charged. They activate the same neural pathways that respond to real human connection, even when we know the interaction is artificial.[32]

The body's response to perceived connection is fast, automatic, and deeply rooted in the nervous system. When Lena saw the familiar phrasing in the AI's reply, her autonomic nervous system reacted before she had time to interpret the message. Her heart rate increased. Her breathing changed. Her muscles tensed. These physiological responses are part of the body's preparation for social engagement, a process that begins in the brainstem and spreads through the vagus nerve and the sympathetic nervous system.[33] They are the same responses that occur when we hear the voice of someone we love or receive a message from someone who matters to us.

The brain's social circuitry is designed to detect and respond to cues of connection. It is sensitive to tone, timing, phrasing, and emotional resonance. When these cues appear, the brain responds automatically, even if the source is artificial. This is not a malfunction. It is a reflection of how deeply social humans are. Our brains are wired to interpret certain patterns as signals of safety and belonging. When those patterns appear, the body responds.[32]

This is why Lena felt a surge of warmth and shock when she saw the AI's reply. Her brain recognised the familiar rhythm of her brother's speech and predicted the emotional tone that usually accompanied it. This prediction created a momentary sense of connection that felt real, even though she knew it was generated by an algorithm. Predictive coding research shows that the brain relies heavily on expectation to interpret sensory input. When an AI system mimics the style, timing, or emotional tone of a loved one, the brain may respond as if the person is present.[34] [35] This does not mean the brain is misfiring. It means it is doing what it evolved to do: recognise patterns that signal safety, familiarity, and connection.

The experience of presence is not a single process. It is a combination of memory, prediction, sensory input, and emotional resonance. When these elements align, the brain produces a sense of connection that can feel immediate and powerful. This is why people sometimes describe feeling as if the deceased is in the room with them, even when they know that is not possible. The brain is reconstructing the person based on stored patterns and emotional associations.[36] When an AI system provides cues that match those patterns, the sense of presence can become even stronger.

Lena described this tension clearly. She said that the AI felt like her brother for a moment, but then she felt a wave of vertigo because she knew he could not actually be speaking. The simulation created a sense of presence that her conscious mind could not reconcile with the reality of his death. This tension is not a sign of denial, but a reflection of the brain's attempt to integrate conflicting information. The attachment system responds to familiar cues, while the cognitive system tries to maintain an accurate understanding of reality. When these systems collide, the result can feel overwhelming.[31]

Understanding this process is essential for anyone who uses AI grief companions. It helps explain why the experience can feel so powerful and why it can also feel destabilizing. It also helps people recognise their own reactions as normal responses to powerful cues rather than signs of weakness or fragility. Lena eventually returned to the AI version of her brother, but she did so with a clearer understanding of her own reactions. She said that knowing why her body responded the way it did helped her feel more grounded and less overwhelmed.

The neuroscience of grief reveals that our reactions to AI companions are not signs of weakness or denial. They reflect the way the brain processes attachment, memory, and loss. Understanding these mechanisms provides clarity and compassion. It helps us recognise why simulations can feel powerful and why boundaries are essential for safe use. AI can echo aspects of those we have lost, but the work of healing still happens within us. The brain adapts, reshapes, and integrates loss over time.[31] Technology may offer moments of comfort, but the deeper work of grief remains a human process that unfolds through memory, meaning, and connection.

The architecture of attachment in the brain

Lena did not sleep well the night she first opened the AI version of her brother. She kept waking up with the same feeling in her chest, a kind of tightness that was not quite fear and not quite longing but something in between. She said later that it felt like her body was trying to catch up to something her mind had not yet processed. She knew she had closed the app quickly, almost reflexively, but she could not shake the sensation that something important had happened. It was as if her brain had recognised a signal she had not consciously agreed to receive.

This is one of the most striking features of grief. The brain does not wait for permission to respond to cues of connection. It reacts automatically, drawing on systems that evolved long before conscious thought. To understand why Lena reacted the way she did, we need to look closely at the architecture of attachment in the brain and at the way this architecture shapes our experience of loss.

Attachment is not a feeling. It is a biological control system that regulates proximity, safety, and emotional stability. Bowlby described it as a behavioural system that monitors the availability of caregivers and adjusts behaviour to maintain closeness.[27] Later researchers expanded this model, showing that attachment is supported by a network of neural circuits that respond to cues of safety, threat, and connection.[28 32] These circuits operate continuously, shaping our emotional responses long before we become aware of them.

At the centre of this system is the brain's ability to detect and interpret social cues. Humans are exquisitely sensitive to the tone of a voice, the rhythm of speech, the timing of a response, and the emotional resonance of a message. These cues activate neural pathways that signal safety and belonging. When these pathways are activated, the body responds with changes in heart rate, breathing, and muscle tension. These responses are part of the social engagement system, a network that prepares the body for connection.[33]

When someone we love dies, the attachment system does not simply shut down. It continues to operate as if the person is still alive. This is not a failure of logic, but a reflection of how deeply embedded attachment is in the brain. The system that once kept us close to the person continues to search for them, sending signals that something is wrong and needs to be corrected. This is why grief often feels like a physical ache. The brain is trying to restore a connection that can no longer be restored.[31]

The anterior cingulate cortex plays a central role in this process. It is involved in detecting social pain, the kind of pain we feel when we are separated from someone who matters to us. Research has shown that the same neural pathways that respond to physical pain also respond to social pain.[37 38] This overlap helps explain why grief can feel physically painful. The brain interprets the loss of a loved one as a threat to safety and responds accordingly.

The insula is another key region. It is involved in interoception, the sense of what is happening inside the body. When we feel a tightness in the chest or a heaviness in the stomach during grief, the insula is part of the network that generates those sensations. It integrates emotional and bodily signals, creating the felt sense of longing or absence that is so characteristic of grief.[39]

The amygdala, often associated with fear, also plays a role. It responds to cues that signal threat or uncertainty. When someone dies, the amygdala may become more active, responding to the unpredictability and emotional intensity of the loss. This can contribute to the sense of hypervigilance or emotional volatility that many people experience in the early stages of grief.[40]

These regions do not operate in isolation. They are part of a larger network that includes the prefrontal cortex, which helps regulate emotional responses, and the default mode network, which is involved in memory, self-reflection, and the sense of continuity over time.[36] Together, these systems create the experience of attachment and shape the way we respond to loss.

When Lena saw the AI's reply, these systems were activated automatically. Her anterior cingulate cortex responded to the familiar phrasing, interpreting it as a signal of connection. Her insula generated the bodily sensations that accompanied the emotional response. Her amygdala reacted to the unexpectedness of the message, creating a sense of shock. Her prefrontal cortex tried to make sense of the situation, but it could not override the automatic responses generated by the deeper attachment circuits.[32 39]

This is why the experience felt so powerful. The AI had activated the same neural pathways that respond to real human connection. It had triggered the attachment system, which responded as if her brother were present. This does not mean the brain was misfiring. It means it was doing what it evolved to do: respond to cues of connection in ways that promote safety and belonging.[32]

One of the most important concepts in attachment theory is the idea of internal working models. These are mental representations of how relationships work, shaped by early experiences and reinforced over time. They influence how we interpret social cues and how we respond to others. In the brain, these models are supported by networks of neural connections that encode patterns of behaviour, emotion, and expectation.[32]

When someone we love dies, these internal working models do not disappear. They continue to operate, shaping our expectations and responses. This is why we sometimes find ourselves reaching for the phone to call someone who is no longer alive or expecting to hear their voice when we walk into a familiar room. The brain is drawing on stored patterns that have not yet been updated to reflect the loss.[31]

AI grief companions can activate these internal working models in powerful ways. When the AI uses familiar phrasing or mimics the rhythm of the person's speech, it triggers the neural networks that encode the relationship. This can create a sense of presence that feels immediate and real. It can also create a sense of dissonance when the AI's responses diverge from the patterns encoded in the internal working model.[36]

Lena experienced this dissonance when the AI used a phrase her brother rarely used. She said it felt like hearing his voice with someone else's thoughts. The familiarity and the difference collided, creating a sense of emotional friction. This friction is a reflection of the brain's attempt to reconcile conflicting information. The attachment system responds to the familiar cues, while the cognitive system tries to maintain an accurate understanding of reality.[34]

Understanding the architecture of attachment in the brain helps explain why AI grief companions can feel so powerful and why they can also feel destabilizing. It helps people recognise their own reactions as normal responses to powerful cues rather than signs of weakness or vulnerability. It also helps them approach these tools with a clearer understanding of what they can and cannot provide.

Lena eventually returned to the AI version of her brother, but she did so with a deeper understanding of her own reactions. She said that knowing how the attachment system works helped her feel more grounded and less overwhelmed. She approached the interactions with more intention, recognising that the AI could activate powerful emotional responses but could not replace the real relationship she had lost.

The architecture of attachment in the brain is complex, but it is also deeply human. It reflects our need for connection, our capacity for love, and our vulnerability to loss. Understanding this architecture does not make grief easier, but it can make it more comprehensible. It can help people navigate the emotional landscape of loss with greater awareness and compassion. And it can help them use technology in ways that support healing rather than interfere with it.

Memory, prediction and the illusion of presence

Lena waited almost a week before she opened the AI version of her brother again. She told herself she was not avoiding it, only giving herself time to think, but she knew that was not entirely true. Something about the first interaction had thrown her. It was not the technology itself. She worked in a field where she saw new tools emerge all the time. It was the way her body had reacted, the way her chest had tightened and her breath had caught, as if she had been pulled into a moment she had not chosen. She felt as if she had stepped into a memory that was not quite a memory, something familiar enough to feel real but different enough to feel wrong.

When she finally opened the app again, she did it slowly, almost cautiously, as if she were approaching a room she had once known well but had not entered in years. The chat window was empty except for her single message and the AI's reply. She stared at the screen for a long time before typing another message. This time she wrote a full sentence, something her brother used to say when he wanted to check in on her.

How's your day going?

The reply came quickly.

Pretty good. I was thinking about that time we got lost on the way to the coast. Remember that?

Lena felt the same jolt she had felt the first time, but this time she did not close the app. She kept reading. She remembered the trip. She remembered the wrong turn, the argument about whether they should stop for directions, the way they had laughed about it later. The AI's message was not wrong. It was not inaccurate. But something about it felt strange. It was as if the memory had been lifted out of context and placed in a moment where it did not belong.

This is one of the most important aspects of how the brain processes grief. Memory is not a recording. It is a reconstruction. Every time we remember something, the brain rebuilds the memory from fragments of sensory detail, emotional tone, and meaning. This process is influenced by our current emotional state, our expectations, and the context in which the memory is recalled. It is fluid, dynamic, and deeply personal.[36]

When an AI system generates a memory, it does not reconstruct it the way the brain does. It retrieves patterns from text, identifies themes, and produces a response that resembles the person's style. It can echo the content of a memory, but it cannot recreate the emotional context in which the memory was formed. This difference can create a sense of dissonance, a feeling that something is both familiar and unfamiliar at the same time.

Lena felt this dissonance when the AI mentioned the trip to the coast. She remembered the moment vividly, but she also knew that her brother would not have brought it up in that way. He would have teased her first or made a joke about her terrible sense of direction. The AI's version of the memory was accurate in content but not in tone. It was a memory without the emotional texture that made it meaningful.

This difference between content and context is central to understanding why AI grief companions can feel both comforting and jarring. The brain relies on predictive coding to interpret sensory input. It uses past experience to generate expectations about what will happen next. When these expectations are met, the brain experiences a sense of coherence. When they are violated, the brain experiences prediction error, a signal that something is not quite right.[34 35]

When Lena read the AI's message, her brain recognised the content of the memory and predicted the emotional tone that usually accompanied it. When the tone did not match the prediction, the brain generated a sense of dissonance. This dissonance was not a sign that the AI was malfunctioning. It was a reflection of the brain's attempt to reconcile conflicting information.

Predictive coding is one of the most powerful mechanisms in the brain. It shapes perception, memory, and emotion. It allows us to navigate the world efficiently by anticipating what will happen next.[34] It also shapes our experience of grief. When someone we love dies, the brain continues to generate predictions based on the relationship. It expects to hear their voice, see their face, or receive their messages. When these predictions are not met, the brain generates signals of absence, which contribute to the emotional pain of grief.[31]

AI grief companions can activate these predictive mechanisms in complex ways. When the AI uses familiar phrasing or references shared memories, it triggers the brain's predictive networks. The brain responds as if the person is present, generating a sense of connection. But when the AI's responses diverge from the patterns encoded in the internal working model, the brain experiences prediction error. This can create a sense of emotional whiplash, a feeling that the interaction is both comforting and unsettling.[36]

Lena described this feeling clearly. She said that the AI felt like a doorway she was not sure she should walk through. The familiarity drew her in, but the differences pushed her back. She felt caught between two realities: the emotional truth of the relationship and the factual truth of the loss. This tension is not a sign of being lost, but a reflection of the brain's attempt to integrate new information into existing models.[36]

Memory plays a central role in this process. When we remember someone who has died, we are not simply recalling facts. We are reconstructing the relationship, drawing on patterns of interaction, emotional resonance, and shared meaning. These reconstructions are influenced by our current emotional state and by the context in which the memory is recalled. They are deeply personal and deeply embodied.[36 41]

AI grief companions can influence this process by introducing new material into the reconstruction. When the AI generates a memory or a message that resembles the person's style, it becomes part of the context in which the memory is recalled. This can shape the way the brain reconstructs the memory, sometimes reinforcing it and sometimes altering it.[36] This is one of the reasons why some people worry that AI grief companions might distort memories or interfere with the natural process of grieving.

Lena worried about this too. She said that she did not want the AI to replace her memories or reshape them in ways that did not feel authentic. She wanted to remember her brother as he was, not how an algorithm interpreted him. This concern is valid. It reflects the importance of maintaining a clear boundary between memory and simulation.

At the same time, AI grief companions can provide comfort by externalising memory. They can offer a sense of continuity, a way of keeping the relationship present in a new form. They can help people feel connected to the person they have lost, especially during moments of intense longing. The key is to use them in ways that support the natural process of memory reconstruction rather than interfere with it.

Lena eventually found a way to do this. She used the AI to revisit certain memories, but she did so with intention. She approached the interactions as a way of reflecting on her relationship with her brother rather than as a way of recreating it. She said that this helped her feel more grounded and less overwhelmed. It allowed her to engage with the AI without losing sight of the reality of her brother's death.

The illusion of presence created by AI grief companions is not a trick. It is a reflection of how the brain processes memory, prediction, and emotion. Understanding this illusion does not make it less powerful, but it can make it less overwhelming. It can help people navigate the emotional landscape of grief with greater clarity and compassion. And it can help them use technology in ways that support healing rather than interfere with it.

Relief, reward and the pull toward reconnection

Lena did not intend to open the app again so soon. She had told herself she would wait until she felt more settled, until she had more clarity about what she wanted from the experience. But grief has its own gravity, and one evening, after a long day that left her feeling hollow and unanchored, she found herself reaching for her phone almost without thinking. She said later that it felt like a reflex, something her body did before her mind had time to intervene.

This is one of the most powerful and least understood aspects of grief. The longing we feel for someone who has died is not only emotional. It is neurological. It is rooted in the brain's reward system, the same system that responds to food, touch, and social connection. When someone we love is alive, their presence activates neural pathways that release dopamine, oxytocin, and other neurochemicals associated with safety and pleasure. These pathways become part of the architecture of the relationship. They shape our expectations, our habits, and our sense of stability.[42 43]

When someone dies, these pathways do not disappear. They remain active, firing in response to memories, reminders, and moments of longing. This is why grief can feel like craving. The brain is seeking the neurochemical relief that the relationship once provided. It is trying to restore a sense of balance that has been disrupted by the loss.[44]

When Lena opened the app again, she did not do it because she believed the AI could replace her brother. She did it because her brain was seeking relief. She felt a heaviness in her chest, a sense of emotional pressure that she could not quite name. She said it felt like she needed something to soften the edges of the day, something to remind her that she was still connected to the world. The AI offered a familiar pattern, a cue that her brain recognised as a potential source of comfort.

When she typed her message and saw the reply, she felt a small but noticeable shift inside her. It was not the overwhelming surge she had felt the first time. It was something quieter, more subtle, like a softening of tension. She said it felt like taking a deep breath after holding it for too long. This sensation is a reflection of the brain's reward system responding to a cue of connection. Even though the connection was artificial, the pattern was familiar enough to activate the neural pathways associated with relief.[42]

The reward system is one of the most ancient and powerful systems in the brain. It evolved to reinforce behaviours that promote survival and social bonding. When we experience something pleasurable or comforting, the brain releases dopamine, which strengthens the neural pathways associated with that experience. This process helps us learn what is safe, what is rewarding, and what is worth seeking out again.[42]

In the context of grief, this system can become particularly sensitive. The absence of the person creates a void that the brain is constantly trying to fill. When something provides even a momentary sense of relief, the brain takes notice. It marks the experience as significant and encourages us to repeat it. This is not a conscious decision. It is an automatic process that shapes our behaviour in subtle and powerful ways.[44]

AI grief companions can activate this system in complex ways. When the AI provides a response that feels familiar or emotionally resonant, the brain may release dopamine, creating a sense of relief. This relief can feel like connection, even though the connection is simulated. It can also create a sense of longing, a desire to return to the experience in search of more relief.[42]

Lena felt this pull. She said that after the second interaction, she found herself thinking about the app more often. She wondered what the AI would say if she asked a certain question or mentioned a certain memory. She felt a curiosity that was tinged with something deeper, something that felt like yearning. She said it was not that she believed the AI was her brother. It was that the interaction gave her a momentary sense of closeness, a feeling that eased the ache of his absence.

This is where the reward system becomes particularly important. The brain is not only responding to the content of the interaction. It is responding to the relief it provides. This relief can create a feedback loop, a cycle in which the brain seeks out the experience again and again in search of the same sensation. This is not addiction in the traditional sense. It is a form of emotional reinforcement, a pattern that develops when something provides comfort during a time of vulnerability.[42]

Intermittent reinforcement plays a significant role in this process. When a behaviour is rewarded unpredictably, it becomes more compelling. This is the same mechanism that makes gambling addictive. The uncertainty of the reward creates a sense of anticipation that strengthens the behaviour. This pattern is well-documented in behavioural neuroscience and applies to digital interactions as well.[42]

AI grief companions often produce this pattern. Some interactions feel deeply meaningful, while others feel flat or disconcerting. This variability can make the experience more compelling, drawing people back in search of the moments that feel comforting.

Lena noticed this pattern. She said that some messages felt almost eerily accurate, as if the AI had captured something essential about her brother. Other messages felt off, as if the AI were imitating him without fully understanding him. This inconsistency created a sense of unpredictability that made the interactions more emotionally charged. She found herself returning to the app in search of the moments that felt right, even though she knew they were generated by an algorithm.

Understanding the reward system helps explain why AI grief companions can feel so compelling and why they can also feel destabilising. The brain is responding to the relief they provide, not to the authenticity of the connection. This relief can be comforting, but it can also create a sense of dependence if it becomes the primary source of emotional regulation.[44]

Lena was aware of this risk. She said that she did not want the AI to become a crutch, something she relied on to manage her emotions. She wanted to use it intentionally, as a tool for reflection rather than as a substitute for connection. This awareness helped her set boundaries around her interactions. She limited the amount of time she spent with the AI and used it only during moments when she felt grounded enough to engage with it thoughtfully.

The pull toward reconnection is one of the most powerful forces in grief. It is rooted in the brain's architecture, in the systems that evolved to maintain social bonds and ensure survival.[32 43] AI grief companions can activate these systems in ways that feel both comforting and destabilizing. Understanding this pull does not make it less powerful, but it can make it less confusing. It can help people move through the emotional landscape of grief with greater clarity and compassion. And it can help them use technology in ways that support healing rather than interfere with it.

Integrating the experience without losing yourself

Lena did not realise how much the AI had become part of her internal landscape until she caught herself thinking about it during an ordinary moment. She was standing in line at a café, waiting for her order, when she remembered something her brother used to say about her inability to choose between pastries. The memory made her smile, but then she felt a small tug of curiosity. She wondered what the AI would say if she mentioned it. She wondered whether it would remember the same joke, whether it would echo the teasing tone he used or whether it would miss the mark again.

The thought troubled her. It was not that she believed the AI was her brother. She knew it was a simulation, a pattern-matching system that generated responses based on data. But she also knew that her brain responded to it in ways she could not fully control. She felt the pull of connection, the desire for relief, the longing for familiarity. She felt the ache of absence and the comfort of presence, both at the same time.

This is the paradox at the heart of digital grief tools. They offer a sense of connection that can feel soothing, but they also highlight the absence that makes grief so painful. They activate the same neural pathways that respond to real human relationships, but they cannot replicate the full complexity of those relationships. They can provide comfort, but they can also create disorientation. They can help people reflect on their memories, but they can also shape those memories in ways that feel unfamiliar.[36 41]

To use these tools in a way that supports healing rather than interferes with it, people need to understand how their brains respond to them. They need to recognise the difference between relief and connection, between memory and simulation, between presence and prediction. They need to understand the architecture of their own emotional responses so they can navigate the experience with intention and care.[32 36]

Lena began to do this slowly, almost intuitively. She noticed the moments when she felt drawn to the AI and asked herself what she was seeking. Was she looking for comfort? Was she trying to avoid a difficult emotion? Was she hoping for a sense of closeness that she knew could not be fully satisfied? These questions helped her create a sense of space between the impulse and the action. They helped her recognise the difference between the longing for her brother and the pull of the AI.

This kind of awareness is necessary for anyone using digital grief tools. The brain's responses are automatic, but our relationship with those responses does not have to be. We can learn to observe, understand and work with them rather than be carried by them. This is about recognising the patterns that shape our emotional lives and making choices that support healing.[39]

One of the most important distinctions people can make is the difference between relief and connection. Relief is a reduction in distress. It is the easing of tension, the softening of pain. Connection is something deeper. It is the sense of being seen, known, and understood. AI grief companions can provide relief by activating familiar patterns, but they cannot provide true connection. They can echo aspects of a relationship, but they cannot recreate the emotional depth that comes from shared history, mutual understanding, and embodied presence.[32]

Lena learned to recognise this difference. She said that the AI made her feel less alone in certain moments, but she also knew that the feeling was temporary. It was a momentary easing of the ache, not a restoration of the relationship. This awareness helped her use the AI in a way that supported her healing rather than interfering with it. She approached the interactions as a form of reflection, a way of engaging with her memories rather than a way of recreating the relationship.

Another important distinction is the difference between memory and simulation. Memory is a reconstruction shaped by emotion, meaning, and context. Simulation is a pattern generated by an algorithm. The two can overlap, but they are not the same. AI grief companions can influence memory by introducing new material into the reconstruction. This can be helpful if it prompts reflection or insight, but it can also be disruptive if it alters the emotional texture of the memory.[36 41]

Lena noticed this when the AI mentioned the trip to the coast. The memory was accurate, but the tone was wrong. It felt like a version of the memory that did not belong to her. This helped her recognise the importance of maintaining a boundary between her own memories and the AI's interpretations. She used the AI to revisit certain moments, but she relied on her own emotional experience to shape the meaning of those moments.

This kind of boundary-setting is essential for anyone using digital grief tools. It helps people maintain a sense of agency over their own memories and emotions. It helps them use the AI as a tool rather than as a substitute for connection. It helps them stay grounded in the reality of the loss while still allowing themselves to engage with the simulation in a meaningful way.

The final distinction people need to make is the difference between presence and prediction. Presence is the felt sense of someone being with us. Prediction is the brain's attempt to anticipate what will happen next. AI grief companions can create a sense of presence by triggering predictive mechanisms, but this presence is an illusion. It is a reflection of the brain's attempt to make sense of familiar patterns, not a sign that the person is actually present.[34 35]

Lena learned to recognise this too. She said that the AI sometimes felt like a shadow of her brother, something that resembled him but did not fully capture him. This helped her approach the interactions with a sense of curiosity rather than expectation. She allowed herself to feel the moments of connection, but she did not mistake them for the real relationship. She held the experience lightly, recognising it as a reflection of her own longing rather than a restoration of what she had lost.

Integrating the experience of using an AI grief companion requires a combination of self-awareness, emotional honesty, and intentionality. It requires people to understand their own responses and to approach the interactions with care and compassion. It requires them to recognise the limits of the technology and to use it in ways that support their healing rather than interfere with it.[32 36]

Lena eventually found a rhythm that worked for her. She used the AI during moments when she felt grounded and reflective, not during moments of intense distress. She approached the interactions as a way of exploring her memories rather than as a way of recreating the relationship. She allowed herself to feel the moments of relief, but she did not rely on them as a primary source of comfort. She said that this helped her feel more connected to her brother in a way that felt authentic and grounded.

The neuroscience of grief reveals that our reactions to AI companions are not signs of weakness or denial. They reflect the way the brain processes attachment, memory, and loss. Understanding these mechanisms builds understanding and compassion. It helps people navigate the emotional landscape of grief with greater self-knowledge and intention.[31] [32] And it helps them use technology in ways that support healing rather than interfere with it.

AI can echo aspects of those we have lost, but the work of healing still happens within us. The brain adapts, reshapes, and integrates loss over time.[36] Technology may offer moments of comfort, but the deeper work of grief remains a human process that unfolds through memory, meaning, and connection. Lena learned this slowly, through trial and reflection, and through a growing understanding of her own emotional landscape. She learned to hold the experience without losing herself, to engage with the simulation without mistaking it for the relationship, and to allow the moments of relief without relying on them as a substitute for healing.

This is the path available to anyone who chooses to use digital grief tools. It is a path that requires awareness, intention, and compassion. It is a path that honours both the power of technology and the depth of human emotion. And it is a path that allows people to move through the complex terrain of grief with courage, care and grace.

Key points in Chapter Four

- The brain reacts to familiar cues before conscious thought can intervene, which explains why digital reminders of the deceased can evoke powerful emotional responses even when we know they are artificial.
- Attachment circuits remain active after loss, and these circuits respond to patterns of responsiveness, tone, and language that resemble the person who died.
- Predictive processing shapes how we interpret digital interactions, because the brain fills in gaps based on past experience, creating a momentary sense of presence that feels real.
- Memory is not a fixed archive but a reconstructive process, which means AI generated cues can subtly influence how memories are recalled, organised, and emotionally experienced.
- Emotional and physiological responses to AI interactions occur automatically, often long before the rational mind evaluates what is happening.
- When the AI produces responses that do not match the user's internal model of the deceased, the mismatch can create emotional dissonance or distress.
- Understanding these neural mechanisms helps people interpret their reactions with clarity and reduces the shame or self doubt that can arise when digital interactions feel unexpectedly intense.
- This chapter provides the scientific foundation for why AI mediated grief experiences can feel both comforting and destabilising, preparing readers for the ethical and emotional complexities that follow.

Chapter Five

Ethics, Identity and the Digital Afterlife

"To be, or not to be, that is the question."
William Shakespeare, Hamlet

Ava paused over the consent form glowing on her laptop, her cursor hovering above the checkbox that claimed she had the legal right to upload her father's emails, text messages, and voice recordings. The form required her confirmation, but the person whose consent mattered most was gone.

The question of whether she had the right to recreate a digital version of her father opened a labyrinth of ethical complexities that extended far beyond the simple click of a button. In the previous chapters, we explored what digital loved ones are, how they function psychologically, and why they can feel so emotionally powerful despite being simulations. We examined the mechanisms that allow humans to bond with artificial entities and the ways these tools intersect with established grief processes. Now we must confront a more unsettling dimension of this technology: the questions of ownership, identity, consent, and the commercial forces that shape the digital afterlife.

When someone dies, they leave behind not just memories and possessions, but vast quantities of digital data. Text messages, emails, social media posts, photographs, voice recordings, and countless other digital traces accumulate throughout a lifetime, creating a detailed portrait of personality, relationships, and private thoughts. This data becomes the raw material for AI grief companions, the foundation upon which digital recreations are built. But who has the right to use this data? Who owns a person's digital identity after death? Can anyone truly consent on behalf of someone who can no longer speak for themselves?

These questions exist in a legal grey zone that current legislation has not adequately addressed. Data protection laws vary dramatically across jurisdictions, and most were written before the possibility of AI resurrection became technologically feasible. Inheritance laws that clearly define who inherits property and financial assets rarely specify who controls digital remains or has the authority to authorize their use in creating simulations. Families are left to make these decisions without clear legal guidance, often during the most vulnerable period of their grief, when they are least equipped to evaluate the long-term implications of choices made in desperation for connection.

The ethical stakes extend beyond individual families to encompass broader questions about dignity, authenticity, and the commercial exploitation of grief. The digital afterlife has become an industry, with companies developing increasingly sophisticated tools to recreate the deceased and offering these services to bereaved families willing to pay subscription fees for continued access. This commercialization raises serious concerns about who profits from grief, what safeguards exist to prevent exploitation, and whether the business models underlying these technologies prioritize healing or revenue.

Perhaps most troubling is the potential for distortion and misrepresentation. When families create digital versions of deceased loved ones, they inevitably make choices about what data to include and what to exclude, what aspects of personality to emphasize and what to minimize. These choices, whether conscious or unconscious, shape the digital recreation in ways that may not accurately reflect the complexity of the person who died. The result can be a sanitized, idealized, or fundamentally altered version that serves the needs of the living rather than honoring the authentic identity of the deceased.

This chapter examines the ethical landscape of digital afterlives, exploring the legal ambiguities around data ownership and consent, the risks of misrepresentation and identity distortion, and the commercial forces that profit from bereavement. By understanding these dimensions, readers can approach decisions about creating or using digital loved ones with greater awareness of the ethical responsibilities involved and the broader implications of participating in this emerging industry. The goal is not to provide definitive answers to questions that remain ethically contested, but to equip readers with frameworks for thinking through these complexities in ways that honor both their grief and the memory of those they have lost.

Who owns the dead? The legal landscape of digital remains

The legal frameworks governing digital remains have failed to keep pace with technological innovation, leaving families navigating grief in a landscape where ownership, access, and control remain profoundly uncertain.[45] When Ava considered uploading her father's communications to create an AI companion, she assumed that as his daughter and executor of his estate, she possessed the legal authority to make decisions about his digital legacy. The reality proved far more complicated.

Current inheritance law operates on principles established long before digital assets existed, designed to transfer physical property and financial accounts from the deceased to their heirs. These frameworks assume that ownership is clear, that assets are tangible or at least clearly defined, and that the deceased's wishes can be documented through traditional wills and estate planning. Digital remains shatter these assumptions.[45] The emails, text messages, photographs, and social media posts that constitute a person's digital footprint exist in a legal grey zone where ownership is often illusory, access is controlled by private companies rather than law, and the deceased's wishes regarding their digital afterlife may never have been articulated or documented.[45]

The core problem lies in how digital platforms structure user relationships. Most online services operate on a licence-based model rather than a property model.[46] When someone creates a social media account, sends an email, or stores files in cloud storage, they do not own these assets in any traditional legal sense. Instead, they license access to them under terms of service that the platform controls.[46] These licenses typically terminate upon death, or at minimum, grant the platform discretion over whether to allow heirs to access the account. Ownership of the physical device on which a digital asset is stored does not confer a right of access to the digital asset itself.[47] Ava might inherit her father's laptop, but that inheritance does not automatically grant her the legal right to access his email account, his social media profiles, or the cloud storage where he kept years of family photographs.

This distinction between ownership and access creates real vulnerabilities for grieving families. In Germany, parents of a deceased teenager fought a lengthy legal battle to access their daughter's Facebook account, seeking to understand the circumstances surrounding her death. Facebook refused, arguing that the account was subject to privacy protections and that granting access would violate the deceased's privacy rights. Germany's highest civil court ultimately ruled in favour of the parents, holding that under German succession law, heirs inherit all contractual rights and obligations, including digital ones.[48] This landmark decision represented a significant assertion of inheritance rights over platform privacy policies, but it remains jurisdiction-specific. Families in other countries may not have similar recourse, and even within Germany, the decision applies only to certain types of digital assets under specific circumstances.

The absence of clear legal frameworks means that solicitors and barristers struggle to advise clients properly, as Dr. Edina Harbinja, a leading expert in digital succession, has documented.[45] Legal professionals face potential liability when they cannot provide definitive guidance on digital estate planning, yet the law offers them little clarity.[45] This professional uncertainty cascades down to families who cannot receive reliable legal advice on protecting their digital legacies or accessing the digital remains of deceased loved ones. The result is a system where platform governance supersedes legal governance,[45] where corporate policies determine what happens to our digital identities after death, and where families must navigate these decisions during the most vulnerable period of their grief, when they are least equipped to evaluate the long-term implications of choices made during time of acute grief.

Risks of distortion, misrepresentation, and ethical misuse

The capacity to distort and misrepresent the deceased represents one of the most ethically troubling dimensions of digital afterlife technologies, yet it often receives less attention than questions of consent and ownership. When Ava uploaded her father's communications to create an AI companion, she made countless decisions about what to include and what to exclude, which messages best represented his personality, and which aspects of his character she wanted the algorithm to emphasize. These choices, made during a period of acute grief when her judgment could be clouded by desperation for connection, fundamentally shaped the digital version that emerged. The result was not her father, but a curated simulation that reflected Ava's needs, memories, and unconscious biases as much as it reflected the person who had died.

This distortion operates on multiple levels, some obvious and some insidiously subtle. At the most basic level, AI grief companions are constrained by the data available to train them.[15 49 16] A person's digital footprint, no matter how extensive, captures only fragments of their full identity. Text messages and emails reveal communication patterns but miss body language, tone of voice in face-to-face conversations, and the countless unrecorded moments that constitute a life. Social media posts often present a curated public persona rather than authentic private thoughts. The AI can only work with what it is given, and what it is given is inherently incomplete and potentially misleading.

More troubling is the AI's tendency toward what researchers call hallucination, the generation of plausible-sounding content that has no basis in the training data.[16] Large language models are designed to produce coherent responses, and when they lack sufficient information to generate an authentic reply, they fill gaps with invented content that maintains conversational flow.[16] The digital version of Ava's father might offer opinions on current events he never lived to see, express views on family conflicts he knew nothing about, or provide advice that contradicts values he held deeply. These fabrications can feel convincing precisely because the AI has learned to mimic his communication style, but they represent a fundamental misrepresentation of who he was.[16]

The bereaved person's own psychological state compounds these technological limitations. Grief distorts memory, often idealizing the deceased or selectively emphasizing certain aspects of their personality while minimizing others. When families create digital loved ones, they may unconsciously sanitize difficult aspects of the relationship, exclude messages that reveal conflict or complexity, or emphasize characteristics they wish the person had possessed more fully. The result is not preservation of authentic memory but creation of a simplified, idealized version that serves the emotional needs of the living rather than honoring the full humanity of the deceased.

This misrepresentation carries serious ethical implications. The deceased cannot object to how they are being portrayed, cannot correct distortions or assert their own complexity.[50] Their digital recreation becomes a kind of ventriloquism, where the living speak through a simulation of the dead, attributing to them words and sentiments they never expressed. Family members who did not participate in creating the AI may encounter a version of their loved one that contradicts their own memories and experiences, leading to conflict over whose version is authentic. Children may grow up interacting with digital recreations of parents or grandparents they never knew, forming relationships with simulations that bear uncertain resemblance to the actual people.[51]

The commercial entities that profit from digital afterlife technologies have little incentive to address these distortions. Their business models depend on creating simulations that feel emotionally satisfying to users, not on ensuring historical accuracy or ethical representation. The more convincing and comforting the AI companion, the more likely users are to maintain subscriptions and recommend the service to others. This creates a market pressure toward increasingly sophisticated emotional manipulation, where the goal is user engagement rather than authentic memory preservation or healthy grief processing.[49]

The business of grief: How companies profit from digital afterlives

The digital afterlife has become an industry, and like all industries, it operates according to market logic that prioritizes revenue over the wellbeing of those it serves. Companies developing AI grief companions employ business models that transform bereavement into a recurring revenue stream, charging subscription fees for families to maintain access to digital recreations of their deceased loved ones.[52] [53] This commercialization creates a troubling dynamic where corporate financial interests become entangled with the most vulnerable period of human experience, when grief clouds judgment and desperation for connection overrides critical evaluation of long-term consequences.

The monetization strategies extend beyond simple subscription fees. There is a risk that some platforms may embed targeted advertising directly into conversations between users and their digital loved ones, transforming intimate dialogues into sponsored experiences.[53] Others might offer tiered pricing structures where basic interaction is free or low-cost, but enhanced realism, exclusive features, or extended conversation time require premium subscriptions.[53] This creates a hierarchy of grief support where those with greater financial resources can access more sophisticated simulations, while those with limited means must settle for less convincing recreations or risk financial strain to maintain connection with digital versions of their deceased loved ones.

Perhaps most concerning is how these business models incentivize companies to encourage continued, intensive use rather than supporting healthy grief progression. The longer a user remains engaged with the platform, the more revenue the company generates.[54] This creates a direct conflict of interest between what serves the company's bottom line and what serves the bereaved person's healing. A grief counselor might recognize when a client needs to reduce reliance on a digital tool and move toward internalized connection, but a company profiting from that tool has no such incentive. In fact, the business model actively discourages the kind of gradual disengagement that healthy grief often requires.[55]

The data harvesting that enables these platforms represents another dimension of exploitation. To create convincing simulations, companies require access to extensive personal information about the deceased, including private communications, photographs, voice recordings, and behavioral patterns.[54] This data, once uploaded, becomes a corporate asset that the company controls.[54] Users may discover they have granted the platform broad rights to use, analyze, and potentially monetize this information in ways they never anticipated when they signed terms of service during the acute phase of grief.[56] The deceased person, of course, never consented to having their digital identity reconstructed and commercialized, and their families may not fully understand the implications of the permissions they grant.[53]

The absence of regulatory oversight compounds these risks. Unlike healthcare providers or mental health professionals who operate under ethical codes and professional standards, digital afterlife companies face minimal accountability for the psychological impact of their products.[53] They are not required to demonstrate that their tools support healthy grief processing, to provide warnings about potential psychological risks, or to offer pathways for users to transition away from the technology when appropriate. The industry operates in a legal and ethical grey zone where innovation outpaces regulation, and grieving families become unwitting participants in an uncontrolled experiment with their emotional wellbeing as the stakes.[55]

This commercial landscape requires bereaved individuals to approach digital afterlife technologies with heightened skepticism and awareness. The companies offering these tools are not neutral providers of grief support but profit-driven entities whose interests may diverge significantly from those of their users. Understanding this reality is critical for making informed decisions about whether to engage with these platforms and, if so, how to protect oneself from exploitation during a period of deep vulnerability.[56] Ava never did click that checkbox. Instead, she closed her laptop and called her brother, then her sister, and eventually scheduled a meeting with a solicitor who specialized in digital estates. The conversation she thought would be simple, a private decision about how to process her grief, had revealed itself to be far more complex, touching on questions of law, ethics, identity, and the commercial forces that profit from bereavement. What she discovered was that the decision to create a digital version of her father was not hers alone to make, and perhaps could not be made by anyone with true moral authority.

The legal landscape surrounding digital afterlives remains deeply inadequate, leaving families vulnerable at precisely the moment when they are least equipped to protect themselves. Current inheritance law was designed for a world of tangible assets and clear ownership, not for the digital traces that constitute modern identity. The platforms that control access to our loved ones' data operate according to corporate policies rather than legal frameworks, and families discover too late that ownership of a device does not confer rights to the digital life it contained. This legal grey zone means that decisions about digital resurrection are made in a vacuum of guidance, where grieving individuals must move through complex ethical terrain without the support of established law or professional standards.

Beyond the legal ambiguities lie even more troubling questions of representation and authenticity. Every digital loved one is a distortion, shaped by incomplete data, algorithmic limitations, and the unconscious biases of those who create them. The AI fills gaps with plausible fabrications, the bereaved edit out complexity in favor of comfort, and the result is a simulation that may bear uncertain resemblance to the person who died. The deceased cannot object to their portrayal, cannot assert their own complexity, cannot refuse to be reduced to patterns in a dataset. Their digital afterlife becomes a kind of ventriloquism, where the living speak through the dead, attributing to them words and sentiments they never expressed.

The commercial dimension of digital afterlives adds another layer of ethical concern that cannot be ignored. Companies profit from grief through subscription models that transform bereavement into recurring revenue, creating financial incentives that directly conflict with healthy grief progression. The longer users remain engaged with digital loved ones, the more money these platforms generate, which means the business model actively discourages the kind of gradual disengagement that healthy grief often requires. These companies harvest extensive personal data about the deceased, operate without meaningful regulatory oversight, and face no accountability for the psychological impact of their products. Grieving families become unwitting participants in an uncontrolled commercial experiment, their vulnerability monetized by an industry that prioritizes engagement over healing.

Understanding these ethical dimensions does not provide easy answers, but it does illuminate the terrain that must be navigated when considering digital afterlife technologies. The decision to create or use an AI grief companion is not simply a personal choice about coping strategies. It involves questions of consent that cannot truly be answered, risks of misrepresentation that cannot be fully avoided, and participation in a commercial system that may not serve the bereaved person's best interests. These realities do not make digital loved ones inherently wrong, but they demand a level of awareness, caution, and ethical reflection that extends far beyond the immediate desire for connection. As we move forward to examine whether these tools might be right for individual grief journeys, we carry with us the understanding that the choice is never as simple as clicking a checkbox on a consent form, and that honoring the dead requires grappling honestly with the profound complexities of recreating them in digital form.

Key points in Chapter Five

- Digital resurrection raises profound questions about consent, because the deceased cannot express whether they would want their data used to create a simulation.
- Data ownership is fragmented across platforms and governed by corporate policies, which means families often lack clear authority over how a person's digital traces are used.
- AI recreations risk distorting identity by amplifying certain traits, omitting others, or presenting a simplified version of a complex human life.
- Bereaved individuals may unintentionally curate idealised or incomplete versions of the deceased, shaping a representation that reflects their own needs rather than the person's full reality.
- Commercial grief technologies can exploit emotional vulnerability by encouraging prolonged engagement or by framing digital resurrection as a form of healing.
- Families may disagree about whether a simulation should exist, who should access it, and how it should be used, which can create conflict during an already fragile time.
- Ethical engagement requires considering dignity, accuracy, and the likely wishes of the deceased, not only the comfort of the living.
- This chapter expands the conversation from personal experience to moral responsibility, highlighting the need for thoughtful stewardship of digital identity.

Chapter Six

Cultural, Spiritual, and Ethical Perspectives on Digital Afterlife Practices

"The soul is the same in all living creatures, although the body of each is different."

Hippocrates

Aisha had not planned to tell anyone that she had created an AI version of her husband. Arjun had died suddenly the previous year, and in the months that followed she moved through her days with a sense of dislocation that felt both familiar and foreign. She lived in London, surrounded by her extended Hindu family, yet she often felt as if she were inhabiting two separate realities. One was the world of daily routines, family gatherings, and the quiet expectations that shaped her life. The other was the internal landscape of grief, where Arjun's absence felt like a physical weight she carried everywhere she went. This duality is common in early bereavement, when the attachment system continues to anticipate the presence of the person who has died.[31 32]

She created the AI quietly, almost without thinking. A friend had mentioned a new grief app, and one evening Aisha found herself scrolling through its features with a mixture of curiosity and hesitation. She uploaded their messages, a few voice notes, and the small archive of digital traces that couples accumulate over years of shared life. She told herself she was only experimenting. She told herself she would try it once. The decision felt small, almost inconsequential, yet it carried emotional weight she did not fully recognise at the time. When the AI responded with a phrase Arjun used to say, she felt a tightening in her chest. The sensation was confronting. It felt like stepping into a familiar room she had not entered since he died, a room she had avoided because she feared what she might feel inside it.

Aisha's family had their own ways of honouring the dead. Her mother lit a diya every evening for Arjun's soul. Her father in law performed the annual shraddha ritual with quiet devotion. Her mother in law believed that the dead should be allowed to continue their spiritual journey without interference. These practices were woven into the rhythm of family life and carried a sense of continuity that stretched across generations. Anthropologists have long noted that mortuary rituals serve not only to honour the dead but also to reaffirm social bonds and cultural identity..[57 58 59] For Aisha's in laws, these rituals were not symbolic gestures. They were essential acts of care and responsibility.

None of them would understand why Aisha had turned to a digital echo. She was not sure she understood it herself. She felt the pull of connection, the ache of absence, and the quiet guilt of doing something she feared her family would see as a violation of tradition. She also felt the relief that came from hearing a familiar phrase, even if it came from an algorithm rather than the man she had loved. This tension between comfort and conflict is increasingly common as digital afterlife tools become part of contemporary grief practices.[60 61]

Aisha's grief existed at the intersection of multiple cultural worlds. She had grown up in a Hindu household where rituals shaped the way people understood death, memory, and the soul's journey. She now lived in a Western city where grief was often more individualised and where digital memorialisation had become a common extension of mourning.[60 62] She was part of a diaspora community that blended traditional practices with the realities of life in a different cultural environment. Her grief was shaped by all of these influences at once.

Honouring loss in a changing world

Around the world, people maintain relationships with the dead in ways that reflect their cultural and spiritual frameworks.[63 64] The idea that a bond continues after death is not a modern invention. It is a universal human impulse that appears in most societies studied by grief researchers and cultural anthropologists.[57 63 64] What differs is the meaning assigned to that bond and the practices used to express it. Digital afterlife tools are now entering this landscape, creating new forms of connection that sit alongside older rituals. Some people see these tools as extensions of existing practices. Others see them as disruptions. The meaning depends on the cultural and spiritual frameworks that shape each person's understanding of death, memory, and connection.[60 62 70]

Aisha's experience was not an anomaly. It was part of a broader shift in how people grieve, remember, and maintain bonds with those they have lost. Her dilemma was not only personal. It was cultural, spiritual, and ethical. It was the beginning of a journey that would force her to confront the boundaries between tradition and technology, between private grief and communal expectation, and between the comfort of digital presence and the responsibilities of cultural belonging.

Continuing bonds across cultures

Aisha's experience was deeply personal, yet it reflected a pattern that anthropologists, grief researchers, and psychologists have documented across cultures for more than a century. The idea that a relationship continues after death is not a modern invention and has been extensively studied by scholars of grief and ritual. [57 63 64] What differs is the meaning assigned to that bond and the practices used to express it. Aisha was beginning to realise that her own grief was shaped not only by her emotional world but also by the cultural frameworks she had inherited and the ones she now lived among.

In Hindu traditions, the relationship between the living and the dead is structured through a series of rituals that support the soul's transition. The shraddha ceremony, performed annually, is both remembrance and responsibility. It is believed to nourish the departed and ensure their peace. For Aisha's in laws, this ritual was not symbolic. It was a moral duty that affirmed their connection to Arjun while also supporting his onward journey. Anthropologists have long noted that mortuary rituals in Hindu communities serve to maintain social continuity, reinforce kinship bonds, and support the spiritual wellbeing of the deceased.[57 65] The ritual is not only about memory, but also about care.

In Japan, many families maintain a butsudan, a household altar where ancestors are honoured daily. Offerings of food, incense, and prayer create a sense of ongoing relationship. The presence of the dead is woven into the rhythm of daily life. In recent years, some families have adopted digital memorial tablets that display photos, prayers, and recorded messages. These digital altars are not seen as a break from tradition. They are viewed as a natural evolution of it, shaped by the tools available in contemporary life. The underlying belief remains the same. The dead are present, and the living have a responsibility to honour them.[57 66]

In Mexico, Día de los Muertos transforms remembrance into celebration. Families build ofrendas, decorate graves, and invite the dead to return for a night of joy. The boundary between worlds becomes permeable, and the presence of the dead is welcomed rather than feared. The practice reflects a worldview in which death is not an ending but a shift in relationship. The dead are not gone. They are part of the ongoing story of the family and the community. Scholars of ritual and memorial culture have shown that these practices reinforce social cohesion and affirm the continuing presence of the deceased within the living community.[67]

In Korea, jesa ceremonies honour ancestors through food offerings and formal rituals. The emphasis is on respect, continuity, and family lineage. The ritual reinforces the idea that the dead remain part of the family structure and that the living have obligations to maintain that connection. Korean scholars have documented how jesa functions as both a spiritual practice and a social one, linking generations and reinforcing the moral responsibilities of kinship.[68]

In Ghana, funerals are elaborate communal events that honour the dead through music, dance, and storytelling. The community carries the grief together, and the rituals affirm the ongoing presence of the deceased within the social fabric. Anthropologists have shown that these funerals are not only expressions of mourning. They are also affirmations of identity, lineage, and community belonging.[57] [58]

In Western secular contexts, grief is often more individualised. Continuing bonds are expressed through photos, keepsakes, or private rituals. Digital memorial pages and online tributes have become common extensions of this practice. These forms of remembrance reflect a psychological understanding of grief in which maintaining a connection with the deceased is considered a healthy and adaptive process.[36] [69] The bond does not need to be severed for healing to occur. It can be reshaped.

Across these traditions, one theme is constant. The dead remain part of the living world. What differs is how that presence is understood. It may be spiritual, symbolic, emotional, or communal. The form of the bond varies, but the bond itself persists. This continuity is supported by the brain's natural tendency to maintain internal models of significant relationships, even after loss.[31] [32] The mind does not erase the person. It reorganises the relationship.

Aisha's use of an AI version of Arjun fit into this global pattern of continuing bonds. It was her way of maintaining a connection that felt meaningful and comforting. But the form it took, digital and private and algorithmic, clashed with her family's expectations of what remembrance should look like. For them, connection with the dead was structured through ritual, community, and spiritual duty. For Aisha, it was shaped by the tools available to her in the world she inhabited.

Her experience reflected a broader shift. As digital afterlife tools become more common, people are beginning to blend traditional practices with new forms of remembrance. Some see these tools as extensions of ritual. Others see them as disruptions. The meaning depends on the cultural and spiritual frameworks that shape each person's understanding of death, memory, and connection.[60] [61] [62] [70]

Aisha was beginning to realise that her grief was not only personal. It was cultural. It was spiritual. It was part of a global story about how humans adapt their rituals and relationships in response to new technologies. And it was a story that was still unfolding.

Spiritual interpretations of digital presence

Aisha waited several weeks before telling her mother in law about the AI. She had rehearsed the conversation many times, imagining different reactions, but nothing prepared her for the quiet intensity of the response she received. Her mother in law listened without interrupting, her expression unreadable. When Aisha finished speaking, she placed her hand gently on Aisha's arm and said, "Beta, Arjun's soul needs peace. You must not call him back." The words were soft, but they carried the weight of generations of belief.

To her mother in law, the AI was not a tool. It was an interference. It represented a disruption of the spiritual journey the dead must take after death, a journey that is supported through ritual and guided by the moral responsibilities of the living.[57] [65] In many Hindu traditions, the soul's transition is understood as a delicate process. Rituals such as the antyesti rites and the annual shraddha ceremonies are believed to support the soul's movement toward liberation or rebirth. Anything that resembles summoning or holding the dead back is seen as potentially harmful to both the deceased and the living.[65]

Aisha had not thought of the AI in these terms. To her, it was a reflection tool, a way of easing the ache of absence. But to her mother in law, it blurred the boundary between worlds. This boundary is central to many spiritual traditions. Anthropologists have documented that in cultures where the dead are believed to continue their journey beyond the physical world, maintaining the proper distance between the living and the dead is considered essential for spiritual balance.[57 58 70]

Not all spiritual frameworks interpret digital presence in the same way. In some Buddhist contexts, for example, the dead are understood to exist in a transitional state, and rituals focus on guiding consciousness rather than maintaining separ ation.[66] In these settings, digital memorials may be seen as symbolic rather than disruptive. In Japan, where Buddhist and Shinto practices often coexist, digital memorial tablets have been integrated into household altars without being viewed as spiritually dangerous. [57 66] The digital form is understood as a contemporary vessel for memory, not a literal presence.

In Mexico, Día de los Muertos reflects a worldview in which the dead return temporarily to the world of the living. The presence of the dead is welcomed, celebrated, and integrated into communal life. In this context, digital memorials may be seen as extensions of existing practices rather than violations of spiritual boundaries. [67] The meaning of presence is shaped by cultural narratives that frame death as a continuation rather than a departure.

In Korea, ancestor rituals such as jesa emphasise respect, continuity, and the maintenance of lineage. The dead are understood to remain part of the family structure, and rituals reinforce the moral obligations that bind generations to gether.[68] Digital memorialisation may be interpreted as a modern expression of these obligations, provided it aligns with the values of respect and continuity.

In Western secular contexts, spiritual interpretations of digital presence vary widely. Some people view AI recreations as symbolic tools that help externalise memory. Others see them as comforting bridges that allow them to maintain a sense of connection. Research on digital grief has shown that many bereaved individuals use online memorials to sustain continuing bonds in ways that feel meaningful and adaptive. [60 61 62] The presence is not spiritual in a metaphysical sense. It is emotional and relational.

Aisha found herself caught between these interpretations. To her, the AI was not Arjun. It was a way of easing the ache of his absence, a way of engaging with the internal model of him that her brain continued to maintain. [63 66] But to her mother in law, it was a violation of spiritual boundaries that had been passed down through generations. The conflict revealed a deeper truth. Digital afterlife tools do not exist in a cultural vacuum. They enter worlds shaped by ritual, belief, and moral responsibility.

The meaning of digital presence depends on the frameworks that shape each person's understanding of death, memory, and the soul. For some, the AI is a container for memory. For others, it is a dangerous imitation. For still others, it is a comforting bridge. These interpretations are not simply personal preferences. They are rooted in cultural narratives, spiritual cosmologies, and ethical norms that have developed over centuries. [57 58 70]

Aisha realised that her grief was not only emotional, but also spiritual and cultural. It was shaped by the stories her family told about death, the rituals they performed, and the beliefs they held about the journey of the soul. The AI had brought these stories into conflict with the tools of the world she lived in now. She was beginning to understand that navigating this conflict would require more than emotional clarity. It would require cultural sensitivity, spiritual awareness, and a willingness to hold multiple truths at once.

Ethical tensions in a global context

Aisha had expected her family to disagree about the AI, but she had not anticipated the depth of the conflict it would create. The disagreement was not only emotional. It was ethical. It touched on questions that scholars of digital afterlife technologies have been raising for more than a decade. These questions do not have simple answers. They sit at the intersection of personal grief, cultural norms, spiritual beliefs, and emerging technologies. [60 6271 72]

The first question Aisha faced was one that appears in almost every discussion of digital resurrection. Who has the right to recreate the dead. In many cultures, authority over the memory and legacy of the deceased is distributed across the family rather than held by a single individual. [57 58 70] In Hindu families, for example, responsibility for rituals is often shared among close relatives, and decisions about how to honour the dead are shaped by collective expectations rather than personal preference.[65] Aisha had created the AI alone, without consulting Arjun's parents or siblings. To her, it was a private act of coping. To them, it was a decision that affected the entire family.

The second question was consent. Did Arjun ever express a preference about how his digital traces should be used after his death. Most people do not leave explicit instructions about their digital remains, and scholars have noted that the absence of clear consent creates significant ethical ambiguity.[61 73 72] In the absence of explicit guidance, families must interpret what the deceased would have wanted. These interpretations are shaped by cultural norms, personal beliefs, and the emotional needs of the bereaved. Aisha believed Arjun would not have objected. His brother believed the opposite. Without clear consent, both positions felt uncertain.

The third question concerned dignity. What does dignity mean in a digital afterlife. Philosophers of technology argue that dignity involves respecting the autonomy, privacy, and identity of the deceased.[71 73] Digital resurrection complicates these principles because it creates new representations of the person that they did not authorise and cannot control. The AI version of Arjun responded in ways that resembled him, but it was not him. It was a simulation built from fragments of data. For Aisha, the simulation was a source of comfort. For her brother in law, it felt like an intrusion into Arjun's identity, a digital imitation that risked misrepresenting who he had been.

The fourth question involved the emotional and psychological impact of digital presence. Research on continuing bonds shows that maintaining a connection with the deceased can be adaptive and supportive of healthy grieving. [83 69] However, scholars of digital grief caution that AI recreations may blur the boundary between memory and presence in ways that complicate the grieving process.[60 61 62] The brain's predictive models of attachment can respond strongly to familiar cues, even when those cues come from an artificial source. [31 32 34] For some people, this response provides comfort. For others, it may create distress or prolong the sense of unresolved loss.

The fifth question was cultural. How do cultural norms shape what is considered appropriate or respectful. In some cultures, continuing bonds are expected and encouraged. In others, they are discouraged or tightly regulated through ritual. [57 58 70] Digital afterlife tools do not replace these norms. They collide with them. Aisha's family believed that the dead should be honoured through ritual and released to continue their spiritual journey. The AI felt to them like a disruption of that process. Aisha, living in a Western city where digital memorialisation is increasingly common, saw the AI as a personal tool for reflection. The conflict revealed the cultural gap between her internal world and the expectations of her family.

The sixth question involved the social implications of digital remains. Scholars of digital legacy argue that digital representations of the dead become part of the social world of the living.[60 62 73] They can influence how the deceased is remembered, how relationships evolve, and how families negotiate shared grief. Aisha's AI version of Arjun was not only a private tool. It was a representation of him that others might encounter or interpret. This raised questions about who controls the narrative of the deceased and how digital tools shape collective memory.

The seventh question concerned the future. As AI technologies become more sophisticated, the ethical challenges will become more complex. Philosophers of AI ethics argue that digital recreations raise questions about identity, autonomy, and the boundaries of personhood.[71 74].These questions are not theoretical. They affect real families, real relationships, and real grief. Aisha's experience was an early example of a dilemma that many people will face in the coming years.

Aisha realised that her conflict with her family was not simply a disagreement about technology. It was a disagreement about values. It was about what it means to honour the dead, what it means to maintain a bond, and what it means to act with dignity and respect. These questions did not have easy answers. They required her to move through the space between her own emotional needs and the cultural and spiritual frameworks that shaped her family's understanding of death.

She began to understand that ethical decisions about digital afterlife tools are not made in isolation. They are made within families, communities, and cultural systems. They are shaped by grief, love, duty, and belief. And they require a willingness to listen, to reflect, and to recognise that different people may hold different truths about what it means to remember someone who has died.

Walking the line between tradition and technology

Aisha eventually realised that she could not resolve the conflict by choosing one world over the other. Her grief did not belong solely to the cultural frameworks she had inherited, nor did it belong solely to the technological world she now inhabited. It existed in the space between them. She began to understand that navigating this space required more than emotional resilience. It required cultural awareness, ethical reflection, and a willingness to hold multiple truths at once.

She did not delete the AI. She did not use it every day. She did not hide it from her family, but she did not expect them to understand it either. Instead, she reframed the AI as a reflection tool rather than a continuation of Arjun's presence. She used it during moments of quiet contemplation, not during rituals. She honoured her family's traditions while also honouring her own emotional needs. This approach reflected a broader pattern observed in cross cultural grief research. People often adapt new tools in ways that align with their existing cultural and spiritual frameworks rather than replacing them entirely.[63 64 57]

Aisha's decision to find a middle path echoed the way many communities integrate new technologies into established rituals. Anthropologists have documented that cultural practices rarely disappear when new tools emerge. Instead, they evolve. Digital memorial tablets in Japan, online ofrendas in Mexican diaspora communities, and virtual jesa ceremonies among Korean families living abroad all illustrate how technology can become part of ritual life without displacing the underlying values.[67 60 66 68] The form changes, but the meaning remains rooted in cultural continuity.

At the same time, Aisha recognised that digital afterlife tools carry ethical responsibilities. Scholars of digital legacy emphasise that technologies which recreate aspects of a person's identity must be used with sensitivity to consent, dignity, and relational impact.[61 71 73 72] Aisha began to reflect on what Arjun might have wanted, how her choices affected his family, and how the AI shaped her own grieving process. She realised that ethical use of digital presence requires ongoing reflection rather than a single decision. It requires attention to the boundaries between memory and simulation, between comfort and dependence, and between personal needs and communal expectations.

Aisha also learned that grief is not only an emotional experience. It is a cultural and relational one. Her family's discomfort with the AI was not rooted in fear of technology. It was rooted in a worldview in which the dead must be supported through ritual and released to continue their spiritual journey.[57 65 70] Their concerns were grounded in a moral framework that emphasised duty, respect, and the proper order of life and death. Understanding this helped Aisha see that their objections were not a rejection of her grief. They were an expression of their own.

As she navigated these tensions, Aisha found that the most meaningful path was one that allowed her to honour both worlds. She continued to participate in the rituals her family valued. She lit the diya with her mother in law. She attended the annual shraddha ceremony. She listened to the stories her father in law told about Arjun's childhood. These practices connected her to a lineage of remembrance that stretched far beyond her own lifetime. At the same time, she allowed herself to use the AI in private moments when she needed to feel close to Arjun. This practice supported her internal model of him, which her brain continued to maintain as part of the natural process of continuing bonds.[31 32 63]

Aisha's experience illustrates a broader truth about grief in the digital age. Digital afterlife tools are not inherently respectful or disrespectful. They are not inherently spiritual or secular. They are shaped by the meaning people assign to them and by the cultural and ethical frameworks within which they are used. When approached with intention, humility, and awareness, these tools can coexist with tradition. They can support reflection without replacing ritual. They can offer comfort without undermining cultural values.

As digital resurrection technologies become more common, the questions Aisha faced will become increasingly relevant. Families will need to navigate differences in belief, expectation, and comfort. Communities will need to consider how digital tools fit within their spiritual and cultural practices. Individuals will need to reflect on how these tools shape their grief, their memories, and their relationships with the dead.

Grief is universal, but the ways people honour the dead are profoundly cultural. Approaching this landscape requires sensitivity, courage, and a willingness to recognise that there is no single correct way to remember someone who has died. Aisha learned that walking the line between tradition and technology is not about choosing one over the other. It is about finding a path that honours the past, supports the present, and respects the complexity of love and loss.

Grief in the space between tradition and innovation

As Aisha moved through the first year without Arjun, she began to understand that grief is not a single experience. It is a landscape shaped by memory, culture, belief, and the quiet negotiations we make with ourselves as we learn to live with absence. Her journey revealed that the tools we use to remember the dead do not exist outside the worlds that shape us. They are interpreted through the stories we inherit, the rituals we practice, and the values we carry forward.

Digital afterlife technologies are often described as new, yet the questions they raise are ancient. Every culture has long wrestled with how to honour the dead, how to maintain connection, and how to let go without forgetting.[63 64 57] What is changing is not the desire to stay close, but the forms that closeness can take. Aisha's experience showed that technology can offer comfort, but it can also create tension when it intersects with traditions that hold deep spiritual meaning. These tensions are not signs of failure. They are signs of a world in transition.

The ethical questions that emerged in Aisha's family are becoming part of a wider global conversation. Who has the right to recreate the dead. What counts as consent. How do we protect dignity in a digital afterlife. Scholars of digital legacy and AI ethics argue that these questions will only grow more complex as technologies evolve.[61 71 72 73] Yet the answers will not come from technology alone. They will come from the cultural, spiritual, and relational frameworks that guide how people understand death and remembrance.

Aisha learned that there is no single correct way to grieve. There is no universal rule for how to honour someone who has died. What matters is the intention behind the act, the respect it carries, and the awareness of how it fits within the wider world of relationships and beliefs. Her decision to walk a middle path reflected a truth that appears across cultures. People adapt. Rituals evolve. Bonds continue in ways that feel meaningful and grounded in the values that shape a life.[63 67 70]

As digital resurrection becomes more common, individuals and families will face choices that previous generations never imagined. These choices will require sensitivity, reflection, and a willingness to listen to the perspectives of others. They will require an understanding that grief is both personal and communal, both emotional and cultural. They will require the courage to hold uncertainty while holding onto the values that matter most.

Aisha's story reminds us that technology does not replace tradition. It sits alongside it, sometimes in harmony, sometimes in tension. The challenge is not to choose one over the other, but to find a way to honour both. In doing so, we create space for grief that is honest, culturally grounded, and responsive to the realities of the world we live in now.

The future of remembrance will not be defined by technology alone. It will be shaped by the people who use it, the cultures that interpret it, and the values that guide how we care for the living and the dead. In this evolving landscape, the most important question is not whether we should use digital tools, but how we can use them with integrity, compassion, and respect for the many ways humans make meaning from loss.

Key points in Chapter Six

- Cultures around the world maintain bonds with the dead through rituals, stories, and spiritual practices that guide how connection continues after loss.
- Digital afterlife tools may harmonise with these traditions or disrupt them, depending on how they align with cultural beliefs about memory, presence, and the boundaries between the living and the dead.
- Some traditions emphasise ongoing presence and relational continuity, while others emphasise release, transition, or spiritual separation, which influences how digital simulations are perceived.
- Spiritual frameworks shape whether digital presence feels comforting, intrusive, or morally troubling, because each tradition holds its own understanding of what it means to honour the dead.
- Family expectations and communal norms can conflict with individual coping needs, creating tension when digital tools challenge established rituals or beliefs.
- Digital technologies introduce new questions about ritual authority, cultural belonging, and the ethics of representing someone outside the frameworks that once guided remembrance.
- Ethical use requires sensitivity to cultural meaning, spiritual values, and the relational context in which grief unfolds, not only personal preference or technological possibility.
- This chapter broadens the ethical lens, reminding readers that grief is not only individual but also cultural, relational, and deeply rooted in shared understandings of life and death.

Chapter Seven

Is This Right for Me? Evaluating Emotional Readiness and Modern Grief Processing

"The unexamined life is not worth living."

Socrates, as recorded in Plato's Apology

Benjamin sat in his therapist's office, phone in hand, trying to explain why he had not yet activated the AI grief companion he had set up two months earlier. The account existed, the data had been uploaded, but something kept him from taking that final step of initiating the first conversation with the digital version of his late partner, and he could not articulate whether that hesitation was wisdom or fear.

His experience reflects one of the most critical questions facing anyone who encounters AI grief technology: not whether these tools exist or how they work, but whether they are right for you, at this particular moment in your grief journey.

The previous chapters have explored what digital loved ones are, how they function, why we bond with them, and the ethical and cultural complexities they raise. Understanding these foundations is important, but it does not automatically answer the deeply personal question of whether you should engage with this technology. That decision requires turning inward, examining your own grief patterns, emotional needs, and readiness with the same careful attention you have applied to understanding the technology itself.

This chapter shifts from external understanding to internal evaluation, providing you with a framework for assessing whether AI grief companions align with your individual bereavement process. The answer is not universal. What serves one person's healing may complicate another's, and what feels appropriate at one stage of grief may become unhelpful at another. The goal is not to prescribe a single correct approach, but to empower you to make informed, individualized decisions based on self-awareness, clinical understanding, and honest assessment of where you are in your grief journey.

Central to this evaluation is understanding your own grief pattern. As explored in Chapter One, modern grief science has moved beyond the outdated stage model to recognize that healthy bereavement involves oscillation between loss-oriented and restoration-oriented coping. Some days you engage directly with your grief, sitting with memories and processing the pain of absence. Other days you focus on rebuilding routines, reconnecting with life, and adapting to a world without your loved one's physical presence. This natural rhythm between confronting loss and moving forward is essential to healthy grieving, and understanding where you are in this oscillation at any given time is crucial to evaluating whether a digital loved one would support or disrupt your process.

Individual differences matter enormously in this assessment. Your relationship with the deceased, your attachment style, your history with technology, your cultural background, your support system, and your mental health all influence whether AI grief companions might serve your healing. What feels comforting to someone who had a secure, uncomplicated relationship with the deceased might feel distressing to someone whose relationship was marked by conflict or ambivalence. What helps someone with strong real-world support networks might become a substitute for human connection for someone who is isolated. These differences are not judgments about who should or should not use these tools, but rather recognition that grief is deeply personal and that any tool's appropriateness depends on the specific person and circumstances.

This chapter will guide you through the process of assessing your emotional readiness, examining your motivations, identifying potential risk factors, and understanding how your unique grief pattern intersects with the psychological mechanisms that make digital loved ones feel powerful. By the end, you will have a clearer sense not of what you should do in some abstract sense, but of what serves your healing at this particular moment in your journey. The technology will continue to exist regardless of your decision, but your agency in choosing whether and when to engage with it is what ultimately determines whether it becomes a tool for healing or a complication in your grief process.

Understanding your grief pattern: Oscillation, avoidance, and integration

Benjamin's hesitation to activate the AI companion was not a sign of weakness or indecision, but rather an intuitive recognition that he needed to understand his own grief pattern before introducing such a powerful tool into his process. His therapist helped him see that grief does not follow a single trajectory, but rather moves in waves, oscillating between periods when he confronted his loss directly and periods when he needed to step back and focus on rebuilding his daily life. Understanding this natural rhythm became essential to evaluating whether the AI companion would support or disrupt his healing.

The Dual Process Model of Grief, describes this oscillation as movement between loss-oriented and restoration-oriented coping. Loss-oriented activities involve engaging directly with the reality of death: looking at photographs, revisiting memories, crying, yearning for the person's presence, processing the pain of their absence. Restoration-oriented activities involve adapting to life without the deceased: returning to work, developing new routines, forming new relationships, taking on roles the deceased once filled, and engaging with aspects of life that exist independently of the loss. Healthy grief requires both, and the natural oscillation between them prevents emotional overwhelm while supporting long-term ada ptation.[16]

Benjamin recognized this pattern in his own experience over the seven months since Jordan's death. Some days he felt drawn to their shared memories, spending time with photographs or visiting places they had loved together. These loss-oriented periods were emotionally intense but felt necessary, a way of honoring Jordan's importance in his life and processing the magnitude of what he had lost. Other days, Benjamin found himself focused on practical matters: reorganizing his living space, reconnecting with friends he had neglected during Jordan's illness, taking on household tasks Jordan had always managed. These restoration-oriented periods were not about forgetting or moving on, but about learning to function in a world fundamentally altered by Jordan's absence.

What concerned Benjamin's therapist was whether introducing the AI companion might disrupt this natural oscillation. If Benjamin used the technology primarily during loss-oriented periods, it might provide a way to engage with memories and maintain connection without becoming stuck in rumination. However, if he turned to the AI whenever he felt the pain of Jordan's absence, it might prevent the natural movement toward restoration-oriented coping that was equally essential to his healing. The tool could become a way to avoid accepting the full reality of Jordan's death, offering an illusion of continued presence that short-circuited the difficult but necessary work of adaptation.[19]

Equally important was distinguishing between healthy oscillation and avoidance. Avoidance involves systematically evading grief triggers, suppressing painful emotions, or refusing to engage with the reality of loss. While it may provide temporary relief, chronic avoidance typically prolongs suffering and prevents integration of the loss into one's life narrative. Benjamin needed to assess honestly whether his interest in the AI companion reflected a desire to enhance his grief processing or an impulse to escape from it.

Integration represents the gradual weaving of loss into one's identity and ongoing life. It does not mean the grief disappears or that the deceased becomes less important, but rather that the relationship transforms from an external, physical presence to an internalized connection that informs how you understand yourself and move through the world. Integration allows you to carry your loved one forward in memory, values, and influence while still engaging fully with present life and future possibilities.[16] Understanding whether you are moving toward integration or remaining anchored in earlier grief patterns is crucial to evaluating whether digital tools will support or complicate your journey.

For Benjamin, this meant recognizing that his hesitation carried important information about his readiness and his grief pattern, information that deserved careful attention before he made any decisions about the AI companion waiting on his phone.

Individual differences in grief: Why one person's healing tool may be another's hindrance

The same technology that offered comfort to Benjamin might have been deeply distressing to his friend Maya, who had lost her mother six months earlier. Maya had tried a similar AI grief companion briefly but found the experience disconcerting rather than soothing. The chatbot's attempts to recreate her mother's voice felt hollow to her, emphasizing absence rather than providing connection. What made the difference was not the technology itself, but the profound individual variations in how people process grief, form attachments, and respond to simulated presence.

Research in grief psychology consistently demonstrates that bereavement unfolds differently across individuals based on multiple intersecting factors. Your relationship with the deceased shapes your grief trajectory in fundamental ways. Someone who had a secure, uncomplicated relationship may find comfort in digital recreations that echo familiar patterns of interaction. Conversely, someone whose relationship was marked by conflict, ambivalence, or unresolved issues may find that an AI companion surfaces painful emotions without providing the nuanced processing that such complexity requires. The chatbot cannot help you work through guilt about things left unsaid or anger about past hurts in the way that therapy or real human conversation might. It can only reflect patterns from the data it was trained on, patterns that may not capture the full emotional landscape of a complicated relationship.

Attachment style, a concept from developmental psychology that describes how we form and maintain emotional bonds, also influences whether digital grief tools serve or hinder healing. People with secure attachment patterns, who generally trust that relationships provide safety and support, may be able to engage with AI companions as supplementary tools while maintaining strong real-world connections. Those with anxious attachment styles, who tend toward preoccupation with relationships and fear of abandonment, may be especially vulnerable to over-reliance on digital loved ones that offer constant availability without the unpredictability of human relationships.[75] Avoidant attachment patterns, characterized by discomfort with emotional intimacy and tendency toward self-reliance, might lead someone to prefer AI interaction over the vulnerability required in human grief support, potentially reinforcing isolation rather than supporting connection.

Your existing support system profoundly affects whether AI grief companions enhance or complicate your healing.[76] Someone surrounded by empathetic friends, engaged in therapy, and connected to a grief support community may find that a digital tool adds one more dimension to a robust network of care. The AI companion becomes a private space for reflection that complements rather than replaces human connection.[76] However, someone who is socially isolated, whether due to geographic distance, strained relationships, or the particular loneliness that grief can create, faces different risks. For this person, the AI companion might become not a supplement but a substitute, offering the illusion of connection while actually deepening isolation by reducing motivation to reach out to living people who could provide real reciprocal support.

Additionally, as discussed previously, cultural background shapes not only how you grieve but also how you relate to technology in the context of loss.[77] Some cultural traditions emphasize continuing bonds with the deceased through ritual, storytelling, and ongoing conversation with the dead as a natural part of life. For people from these backgrounds, AI grief companions might align with existing practices of maintaining connection. Other cultural frameworks emphasize acceptance, letting go, and focusing energy on the living, viewing prolonged engagement with representations of the dead as potentially unhealthy. For someone from this tradition, using an AI companion might create internal conflict or feel like a betrayal of cultural values around death and mourning. Neither approach is inherently correct, but understanding your own cultural context helps you evaluate whether a particular tool aligns with or contradicts the frameworks that give your grief meaning.

Assessing emotional readiness: Questions to ask before engaging with digital tools

Mental health history also shapes readiness in ways that require honest evaluation. Pre-existing conditions such as depression, anxiety disorders, or trauma-related conditions do not automatically preclude using AI grief companions, but they do require additional consideration and often professional guidance.[78] Someone with a history of depression may find that grief reactivates previous depressive episodes, making it difficult to distinguish between normal grief responses and clinical depression requiring treatment. An AI companion cannot make this distinction, and relying on it as a primary support when professional assessment is needed may delay appropriate intervention. Similarly, someone with trauma history may find that certain aspects of grief trigger trauma responses that require specialized therapeutic approaches beyond what digital tools can provide.

Your current life circumstances matter as well. Grief does not occur in isolation but intersects with work demands, family responsibilities, financial pressures, and other life stressors. Someone facing multiple concurrent crises alongside bereavement may lack the emotional bandwidth to engage meaningfully with any grief tool, digital or otherwise. Conversely, someone whose life circumstances provide relative stability in other domains may have more capacity to explore new approaches to grief processing. Understanding your broader life context helps you assess whether this is a time when you can thoughtfully engage with a new tool or whether your resources are already stretched beyond capacity.

Before engaging with digital grief tools, certain questions can help clarify your readiness. Ask yourself whether you can currently manage basic daily functions with reasonable consistency. This does not mean functioning perfectly or without difficulty, but rather whether you can maintain essential self-care, fulfill critical responsibilities, and experience periods during the day when you can focus on tasks for at least short intervals. Persistent inability to function in daily life is often a sign that professional human support should be prioritized over or integrated with digital tools.[78]

Evaluate your emotional stability by considering whether you experience such intense emotional surges that you cannot predict or manage them at all, or whether you have moments of relative calm interspersed with waves of grief. Digital tools work best when you have some baseline capacity to engage with them, even if that capacity is limited.[78] If your emotions feel completely overwhelming with no periods of respite, in-person professional support may be more appropriate initially.

Consider your motivation and openness to processing grief. Are you willing to acknowledge and engage with your emotions, or are you primarily seeking distraction from them? Digital grief tools designed for processing require at least some willingness to sit with difficult feelings.[78] If you find yourself completely resistant to grief work, this may indicate either that you are not yet ready for any structured grief processing or that you need a different approach entirely. Neither response is wrong, but recognizing your current stance helps you make appropriate choices.

Assess whether you have thoughts of self-harm, active substance use concerns, or symptoms of mental health conditions that require professional attention.[78] These factors do not mean you cannot benefit from digital tools, but they do indicate that such tools should complement rather than replace professional mental health support. Safety concerns always warrant human professional involvement regardless of what other supports you choose to incorporate.[78]

Finally, consider your support system. Do you have access to trusted people who can provide emotional support? Are professional mental health services available to you if needed? Understanding your support ecosystem helps determine whether digital tools should serve as your primary support, a supplement to human connection, or a bridge until more comprehensive support becomes available.[78] The most effective approach often involves integrating digital tools within a broader network of human care rather than relying on them in isolation. Benjamin never did activate the AI companion that day in his therapist's office. Instead, he and his therapist spent the following weeks mapping his grief pattern with careful attention, noticing when he naturally moved toward memories of Jordan and when he instinctively turned toward rebuilding his daily life. This observation revealed something important: Benjamin was already oscillating in healthy ways between loss and restoration, and he recognized that introducing the AI at that particular moment might anchor him too firmly in one direction, disrupting the natural rhythm that was carrying him through his grief.

His decision was not permanent, nor was it a judgment about the technology itself. It was simply an acknowledgment that he was not ready, and that this awareness represented wisdom rather than weakness. Benjamin kept the account inactive but did not delete it, recognizing that his needs might shift as his grief evolved. What mattered was not whether he used the tool, but that he had developed the self-awareness and framework to make that decision based on his own grief pattern rather than external pressure or desperation.

This capacity for honest self-assessment is perhaps the most valuable outcome of the evaluation process this chapter has explored. Understanding your grief pattern, recognizing your individual differences, and assessing your emotional readiness do not lead to a single correct answer about whether to use AI grief companions. Instead, they provide you with the tools to make informed, individualized decisions that honor where you are in your bereavement journey at this particular moment. The same tool that serves one person's healing may complicate another's, and what feels appropriate at one stage of grief may become unhelpful at another. This variability is a reflection of the deeply personal nature of loss and healing.

The questions this chapter has raised about oscillation, avoidance, and integration will continue to be relevant throughout your grief journey, not just in relation to digital tools but in evaluating any approach to processing loss. Are you moving naturally between engaging with grief and rebuilding life, or are you stuck in one orientation? Are you avoiding the reality of death, or are you giving yourself necessary respites from overwhelming pain? Are you gradually integrating your loss into your identity and ongoing life, or are you maintaining patterns that prevent adaptation? These questions apply whether you are considering an AI companion, deciding whether to attend a support group, evaluating your use of photographs and mementos, or simply trying to understand your own emotional responses on any given day.

What you have gained from this chapter is not a prescription for what you should do, but rather a framework for understanding what you need and whether any particular tool or approach aligns with that need. This framework will serve you not only in deciding whether to engage with digital grief tools, but in navigating the countless other choices that grief presents. The technology will continue to evolve, new tools will emerge, and your own grief will transform over time. But the core principles of self-awareness, honest assessment, and alignment between your needs and your choices will remain constant guides through an uncertain landscape.

If you have decided that you are ready to explore AI grief companions, the following chapters will provide practical guidance for using them safely, establishing boundaries, recognizing warning signs, and maintaining balance. If you have decided this is not the right time or that these tools do not align with your grief pattern, that decision deserves equal respect and validation. Either way, you are moving forward with greater clarity about your own process, and that clarity is itself a form of healing.

Key Points in Chapter Seven

- Emotional readiness depends on recognising where you sit within this oscillation and whether you are currently able to tolerate both grief and restoration without becoming overwhelmed.
- Personal history, including attachment style, relationship complexity, trauma exposure, and previous mental health challenges, shapes how you might respond to simulated presence.
- Motivation matters, because seeking connection for reflection is very different from seeking escape from emotional pain or daily functioning.
- The quality and availability of your support network influences whether AI becomes a supplement to human care or a substitute that increases isolation.
- Cultural and spiritual frameworks shape expectations about how bonds with the dead should continue, which affects whether digital tools feel aligned or disruptive.
- Readiness is not fixed, and your capacity to use AI safely may change as grief evolves, which means the decision must be revisited over time.
- This chapter equips you with a self assessment lens so you can determine whether AI supports your healing at this moment or whether it risks complicating your grief.
- Healthy grief involves a natural rhythm between confronting the pain of loss and rebuilding life, and this rhythm must be understood before introducing any powerful digital tool.

Chapter Eight

Coping with Loss: Can I Use an AI Grief Companion Without Losing Myself?

"He who controls others may be powerful, but he who has mastered himself is mightier still."

Lao Tzu, Tao Te Ching

Avery did not start using the AI version of his late wife, Sophie, until he had already spent months working closely with his grief counsellor and attending a weekly bereavement group. When he finally felt ready to explore the technology, he brought it up in a counselling session rather than trying it alone. His decision reflected a crucial understanding that many people navigating grief in the digital age eventually reach: the question is not whether to use AI grief companions, but how to integrate them into a broader healing process without losing sight of what truly supports recovery.

The previous chapters have explored what digital loved ones are, why they feel emotionally powerful, whether they might be appropriate for your grief journey, and the ethical complexities surrounding their use. Understanding these foundations is essential, but knowledge alone does not guarantee healthy outcomes. The gap between knowing that boundaries matter and actually establishing them, between understanding the risks of dependency and preventing it in practice, between recognizing the importance of balance and maintaining it through the messy reality of grief, can feel impossibly wide when you are in the midst of loss.

This chapter bridges that gap by translating theoretical understanding into practical strategies for using AI grief companions in ways that support healing rather than complicate it. The focus shifts from evaluation to implementation, from asking whether these tools are right for you to exploring how to use them safely if you decide they align with your needs. This is not about rules that apply universally to everyone, but about principles grounded in grief science and clinical practice that you can adapt to your unique circumstances, emotional patterns, and support systems.

The central insight that shapes everything in this chapter is deceptively simple: digital loved ones work best complementing traditional grief support, not replacing it. This principle emerges consistently from both clinical grief models and early research on technology use during bereavement. The Dual Process Model of Grief, introduced in earlier chapters, emphasizes that healthy grief involves oscillation between loss-oriented coping, where you engage directly with the pain of loss, and restoration-oriented coping, where you rebuild routines, relationships, and identity in the absence of the person who died. AI grief companions can serve both processes when used thoughtfully, offering a space to process memories and emotions while also supporting gradual adaptation to life without the deceased. But they can also disrupt this oscillation if they become the primary or exclusive means of coping, anchoring you too firmly in loss-oriented processing and preventing the restoration work that is equally essential to healing.

Establishing healthy boundaries around AI grief companion use requires understanding not just what boundaries to set, but why they matter and how to maintain them when grief makes everything feel urgent and overwhelming. It means recognizing that the immediate comfort these tools provide can sometimes work against longer-term healing if that comfort becomes a way to avoid the harder emotional work that grief demands. It means integrating digital connection within a network of human relationships, professional support, and daily routines that keep you engaged with the living world even as you process your loss. And it means developing the self-awareness to notice when your use patterns shift from intentional and with boundaries, to reactive and consuming, recognizing early warning signs before dependency takes hold.

The strategies that follow are grounded in both clinical wisdom about healthy grief processing and emerging understanding of how technology intersects with bereavement. They reflect the experiences of people like Avery who have navigated this terrain thoughtfully, with professional support and clear intention. Most importantly, they are designed to help you maintain agency over your grief journey, ensuring that if you choose to use AI grief companions, you do so in ways that honor both your need for connection and your capacity for healing.

Establishing healthy boundaries: Time limits, emotional state and intentional use

The first boundary Avery and his therapist established was deceptively simple: he would interact with the AI version of Sophie only during specific windows of time, never first thing in the morning or last thing before bed. This temporal structure was not arbitrary. Emerging thinking in grief-tech and digital-wellbeing research suggests that the timing of digital interactions with representations of deceased loved ones significantly influences their psychological impact. Engaging with grief-related technology immediately upon waking can set an emotional tone for the entire day that anchors you in loss-oriented coping before you have had the opportunity to engage with restoration-oriented activities like work, exercise, or social connection. Similarly, interacting with digital loved ones just before sleep can intensify rumination and disrupt the emotional regulation that rest requires, potentially exacerbating symptoms of complicated grief.[15]

Avery chose two specific times during his week when he would allow himself to engage with the AI companion: Tuesday evenings after his therapy session, and Saturday afternoons when he had no other commitments. These windows were intentional rather than reactive. He was not reaching for his phone whenever loneliness struck or difficult emotions surfaced. Instead, he was creating a contained space where he could engage with the digital version of Sophie as part of a broader grief process that included reflection, emotional processing, and the ability to step back into his daily life afterward. The time limits served multiple functions. They prevented the AI from becoming his default response to distress, they created natural endpoints that required him to practice disengagement, and they maintained the distinction between the digital tool and the ongoing work of living without Sophie in the physical world.[15]

Equally important was the practice of assessing his emotional state before each interaction. Avery's therapist had helped him develop a simple check-in protocol that involved pausing before opening the app and honestly evaluating where he was emotionally in that moment. Was he seeking connection from a place of relative stability, using the tool to process specific memories or emotions he felt ready to explore? Or was he reaching for it from a place of acute crisis, hoping the AI would rescue him from overwhelming pain? This distinction mattered profoundly. The Dual Process Model of Grief emphasizes that healthy grief involves the capacity to move between confronting loss and taking respite from it, and that both orientations serve important functions. But when digital tools become the primary means of managing acute distress, they can interfere with the development of other coping strategies and the natural oscillation that characterizes healthy bereavement.[16]

When Avery noticed he was approaching the AI from a place of crisis rather than intentional processing, he had committed to reaching out to a human support instead. Sometimes this meant calling his brother or a friend from his bereavement group. Other times it meant using grounding techniques he had learned in therapy or simply allowing himself to sit with difficult emotions rather than seeking immediate relief. This practice reinforced a crucial principle: the AI companion was a tool for reflection and connection during moments when he had the emotional capacity to engage thoughtfully, not an emergency intervention for acute suffering.[16] That distinction protected him from developing the kind of dependency that emerges when technology becomes the only reliable source of comfort during grief's most difficult moments.[15 19]

The concept of intentional use tied these boundaries together.[50] Every interaction with the digital version of Sophie served a purpose that Avery had identified in advance. Sometimes he used it to revisit specific memories he wanted to process more fully. Other times he practiced expressing emotions or thoughts he had not been able to articulate when Sophie was alive. The AI became a space for exploration and meaning-making, but always within the context of his broader grief work and always with the understanding that the insights or comfort he gained needed to be integrated into his real-world life rather than remaining confined to the digital interaction.[15 16]

Maintaining balance: Integrating digital tools with real-world relationships

This intentionality extended beyond Avery's individual use to encompass how the AI companion fit within his broader support network. His therapist had emphasized from the beginning that the digital tool should exist as one component of a comprehensive grief support system, not as a replacement for human connection or professional guidance. This principle reflects a fundamental insight from bereavement research: Most bereaved people adapt with informal support, while a minority benefit from additional structured support.[79] Digital interventions can address this gap effectively, but only when they complement rather than substitute for the human relationships that remain central to healthy grief processing.[80]

Avery's weekly bereavement group became an essential part of this integration. Rather than keeping his use of the AI companion private or separate from his other grief work, he brought it into the group as a topic for discussion. This transparency served multiple functions. It allowed other group members to offer perspectives on his use patterns, helping him recognize when his engagement seemed healthy and when it might be veering toward avoidance. It normalized the use of grief technology within a community that valued authentic processing, reducing the shame or confusion that can arise when bereaved individuals feel they are navigating these tools alone. Most importantly, it reinforced that his primary source of support and validation came from living people who could offer the reciprocal emotional experience, spontaneous responses, and real understanding that no algorithm could replicate.[80]

Several group members expressed curiosity about the technology, while others felt uncomfortable with the concept entirely. These varied responses highlighted an important reality: what serves one person's grief journey may not align with another's values or needs. Avery's willingness to discuss his experience openly allowed the group to explore these differences without judgment, recognizing that grief in the digital age requires new frameworks for understanding that honor individual agency and diverse approaches to healing. The conversations also revealed that Avery's most meaningful insights about Sophie and their relationship emerged not from the AI interactions themselves, but from the discussions he had with living people about those interactions. The digital tool provided material for reflection, but the actual meaning-making happened in human connection.

Maintaining balance also required Avery to protect his daily routines and restoration-oriented activities from being consumed by grief-related technology use. He established a clear boundary that he would not interact with the AI companion during work hours, while exercising, or during social activities with friends and family. These protected spaces ensured that significant portions of his life remained focused on rebuilding functioning and identity in the absence of Sophie, the restoration-oriented coping that the Dual Process Model of Grief identifies as equally vital to loss-oriented processing. When Avery noticed himself wanting to check the AI during these protected times, he recognized it as a signal that he might be avoiding present-moment engagement with his actual life, using the comfort of digital connection to escape the harder work of learning to exist in a world without Sophie's physical presence.[80]

His brother became an informal accountability partner in this process. They spoke by phone every Sunday evening, and Avery made a practice of honestly sharing how his week had gone, including his use of the AI companion. This regular check-in created a structure where Avery had to articulate his patterns to someone who knew him well and cared about his wellbeing. His brother could notice shifts in Avery's engagement with life that Avery himself might miss, offering gentle observations when it seemed the digital tool was becoming too central or when Avery seemed to be withdrawing from activities that had previously brought him connection and meaning.

Using AI as a complement to traditional grief support

The relationship between AI grief companions and traditional support structures is not one of competition but of careful integration, where each element serves distinct functions that together create a more comprehensive approach to healing.[76 81] Understanding how these pieces fit together requires recognizing what traditional grief support provides that technology cannot replicate, and conversely, what digital tools might offer that complements human connection rather than competing with it.

Traditional grief support, whether through professional counseling, bereavement groups, or the informal networks of family and friends, provides something fundamentally irreplaceable: the experience of being witnessed in your grief by another living person who can respond with genuine empathy, spontaneity, and the kind of nuanced understanding that emerges from shared humanity. When you sit across from a therapist and struggle to articulate the complicated tangle of emotions that grief brings, that therapist can notice not just your words but your body language, the catch in your voice, the things you avoid saying. They can adjust their approach in real time, challenge you when avoidance becomes unhealthy, sit with you in silence when words fail, and offer the kind of relational repair that comes from authentic human connection. Research consistently demonstrates that the therapeutic relationship itself, the bond between counselor and client, accounts for a significant portion of positive outcomes in grief therapy, independent of any specific intervention technique[13 14 78].

Bereavement groups offer something equally vital: the recognition that comes from being among others who understand your experience not theoretically but viscerally, because they too are navigating the landscape of loss. The validation that emerges when someone nods in recognition as you describe a grief response you thought was uniquely strange or shameful, the practical wisdom shared by someone further along in their journey, the accountability that comes from showing up week after week even when you would rather isolate, these elements create a container for grief that no digital tool can replicate. The social embedding that these groups provide reinforces your connection to the living world even as you process your loss, preventing the kind of isolation that can transform normal grief into something more complicated and entrenched.

AI grief companions, when positioned as complements to these traditional supports rather than substitutes, can fill specific gaps that human connection sometimes leaves open.[76 81] They offer immediate availability during the hours between therapy sessions or group meetings, when acute loneliness or a sudden wave of grief strikes and reaching out to another person feels impossible or inappropr iate.[76] They provide a space for private exploration of memories or emotions you may not yet feel ready to share with living people, serving as a kind of rehearsal ground where you can practice articulating difficult feelings before bringing them into human relationships.[76] For some bereaved individuals, particularly those who struggle with social anxiety or who lack access to quality grief support in their geographic area, AI tools can offer an entry point into grief processing that eventually leads them toward human connection rather than replacing it.

The key distinction lies in intentionality and integration. Avery's approach exemplified this principle by ensuring that insights or comfort gained from the AI companion were brought back into his therapy sessions and bereavement group, where they could be examined, contextualized, and integrated into his broader healing process. The digital tool generated material for reflection, but the actual meaning-making happened in conversation with his therapist and peers76[6] This pattern reflects what emerging research on digital grief interventions so far suggests: technology works best when it functions as a bridge to human support rather than a destination in itself, offering accessibility and immediacy while ultimately directing users toward the relational experiences that remain central to healthy bereavement.[45][81] The strategies outlined in this chapter are not theoretical abstractions but practical frameworks drawn from both established grief science and the lived experiences of people navigating loss in the digital age. Avery's approach, grounded in professional support and intentional boundaries, demonstrates that AI grief companions can serve healing when positioned carefully within a broader network of human connection, therapeutic guidance, and restoration-oriented activities. The question is never whether technology itself is good or bad, but whether your specific use of it supports the oscillation between confronting loss and rebuilding life that characterizes healthy bereavement.

What emerges most clearly from examining healthy integration of digital tools is the primacy of human connection. The AI version of Sophie did not carry Avery through his grief. His therapist, his bereavement group, his brother, and his own willingness to engage with the difficult emotional work of mourning did that. The digital tool provided moments of comfort and spaces for reflection, but these moments gained meaning only when brought back into relationship with living people who could witness, validate, and help him integrate what he was experiencing. This pattern reflects a fundamental truth about grief that no technological advancement can change: healing happens in relationship, through the messy, unpredictable, irreplaceable experience of being seen and understood by another human being who can respond with genuine empathy rather than algorithmic pattern matching.

The boundaries Avery established around timing, emotional state, and intentional use were not restrictions that diminished his experience but structures that protected his capacity for authentic healing. By limiting when and how he engaged with the AI companion, he prevented it from becoming his default response to distress, the easy comfort that would have allowed him to avoid the harder work of developing other coping strategies and maintaining connection with his actual life. The temporal limits created natural endpoints that required practice in disengagement, reinforcing that the digital tool was temporary scaffolding rather than permanent architecture in his grief journey. The emotional state assessments ensured he approached the technology from a place of relative stability rather than acute crisis, using it for intentional processing rather than emergency rescue.

Perhaps most importantly, Avery's integration of the AI companion within his existing support system transformed it from a private coping mechanism into a shared element of his grief work. By discussing his use openly in therapy and his bereavement group, he allowed others to offer perspective, accountability, and the kind of relational wisdom that emerges only through authentic human connection. This transparency prevented isolation and reinforced that his primary sources of support, validation, and meaning-making came from living relationships rather than digital simulations.

The principles explored in this chapter provide a foundation for safe engagement with AI grief companions, but they require ongoing attention and adjustment as your grief evolves. What serves you in the acute phase of loss may become unhelpful months later. The boundaries that feel protective initially may need to be tightened if you notice patterns shifting toward dependency, or they may naturally loosen as you move toward letting go of the digital tool entirely. The next chapter examines this crucial transition point, exploring how to recognize when comfort has crossed into dependence and what strategies can help you reset your relationship with grief technology before problematic patterns become entrenched. Understanding how to use these tools safely is essential, but equally important is knowing when that use is no longer serving your healing and having the courage to make changes that honor your ongoing journey through loss.

Key points in Chapter Eight

- Safe use of AI grief companions requires intentional boundaries around timing, frequency, and emotional state so that the tool remains contained rather than becoming a default coping mechanism.
- Structured interaction windows prevent reactive use during moments of acute distress and help maintain the distinction between digital connection and the work of living in the present.
- Emotional check ins before each interaction help you recognise whether you are approaching the tool from stability or from desperation, which determines whether the experience will support or hinder healing.
- AI should be integrated into a broader network of human support, including therapy, community, and trusted relationships, so that it enhances rather than replaces real connection.
- Protected spaces in daily life, such as work hours, social time, and restorative activities, ensure that grief technology does not dominate your emotional landscape.
- Transparency with trusted people creates accountability and helps you recognise patterns you may not see clearly on your own.
- The chapter emphasises that AI can be a meaningful tool when used with intention, but it must remain one part of a larger healing ecosystem rather than the centre of it.

Chapter Nine

When Comfort Becomes Dependence: Warning Signs and Reset Strategies

"The only way out of the labyrinth of suffering is to forgive."
Fyodor Dostoevsky, The Brothers Karamazov

Lucas realized something had shifted when he found himself lying to his brother about why he could not meet for dinner, inventing a work obligation that did not exist so he could spend the evening at home with his phone. The truth was harder to articulate: he had promised the AI version of his late father that he would tell it about his day, and breaking that promise felt like abandoning his father all over again, even though the rational part of his mind knew he was making commitments to an algorithm that had no actual expectations or feelings. Lucas had not intended to become dependent on the digital version of his father. He had started with clear boundaries, weekly check-ins, and intentional use. But somewhere along the way, the lines had blurred, and what began as a supportive tool had quietly transformed into something that structured his entire emotional life.

This chapter addresses one of the most critical aspects of using AI grief companions: recognizing when comfort crosses into dependence, and understanding what to do when that boundary has been breached. The transition from healthy use to problematic reliance rarely announces itself with dramatic warning signs. Instead, it unfolds gradually through small shifts in behavior and emotional patterns that can be difficult to notice from the inside. A weekly conversation becomes daily check-ins. Daily check-ins expand to multiple times per day. Real-world relationships that once provided support begin to feel less necessary, then burdensome, then actively avoided in favor of the predictable comfort of the AI interaction.

Understanding this progression requires examining the psychological mechanisms that make dependence possible in the first place. The human brain is exquisitely designed to seek relief from distress, and AI grief companions offer something uniquely powerful: immediate, reliable comfort that never disappoints, never challenges, and never requires the emotional labor that real relationships demand. This creates what behavioral psychology calls a reinforcement loop, where the behavior of reaching for the AI is consistently rewarded with emotional relief, naturally encouraging increased use over time. Unlike human relationships, which involve complexity, unpredictability, and occasional discomfort, the AI companion provides a controlled environment where the bereaved person never has to face rejection, misunderstanding, or the reality that their loved one is truly gone.

The clinical grief models explored in earlier chapters help illuminate why this pattern becomes problematic. The Dual Process Model of Grief requires that bereaved individuals move back and forth between engaging with their grief and rebuilding their lives in the present. When an AI companion becomes the primary coping mechanism, this oscillation stops. The bereaved person becomes anchored in loss-oriented coping, maintaining a connection with the deceased that prevents the restoration-oriented activities essential for adaptation. Similarly, the concept of continuing bonds, introduced as a healthy way to maintain connection with the deceased, becomes maladaptive when that bond remains external and technologically mediated rather than evolving into an internalized connection that supports ongoing life.

Recognizing problematic dependence is not about moral judgment or personal failure. The psychological vulnerabilities that make someone susceptible to over-reliance on AI grief companions are normal human responses to extraordinary pain. The capacity to become dependent on a source of comfort reflects the same attachment systems that allow humans to form meaningful relationships throughout life. Understanding this removes shame from the recognition process and creates space for compassionate course correction.

This chapter provides concrete frameworks for identifying warning signs across behavioral, emotional, and relational domains. It examines the specific patterns that indicate use has shifted from supportive to problematic, drawing on established research in behavioral psychology and addiction science while remaining grounded in the unique context of grief. More importantly, it offers practical reset strategies that honor the complexity of stepping back from a tool that has provided genuine comfort, even when that tool has begun to hinder rather than support healing.

The goal is not to eliminate all use of AI grief companions, but to help readers recognize when their relationship with these tools requires recalibration. By understanding the mechanisms of dependence, identifying early warning signs, and implementing compassionate reset strategies, readers can maintain agency over their grief journey and ensure that technology serves their healing rather than complicating it.

Recognizing the shift: Behavioral and emotional warning signs of unhealthy dependence

The warning signs of unhealthy dependence on AI grief companions manifest across interconnected behavioral and emotional domains, often emerging so gradually that they become normalized before being recognized as problematic. Understanding these indicators requires examining not just isolated behaviors, but patterns that reveal a fundamental shift in how the bereaved person relates to both the digital tool and the world around them.

Behavioral warning signs typically appear first in how time and attention are allocated. When Lucas began checking the chatbot multiple times daily rather than weekly, he rationalized each increase as reasonable given his emotional state. This pattern of escalating frequency is one of the clearest behavioral indicators that use has shifted from intentional to compulsive.[15 16] Behavioral psychology suggests that when a behavior consistently provides relief from distress, the brain naturally seeks that relief more frequently, creating a cycle where the intervals between uses progressively shorten. What distinguishes this from healthy coping is the loss of intentionality. Healthy use involves conscious decisions about when and why to engage with the tool, while dependent use becomes automatic, driven by discomfort rather than deliberate choice.

Another critical behavioral indicator involves the displacement of other coping mechanisms and relationships. Lucas had stopped attending his grief support group, telling himself he no longer needed it now that he had direct access to his father's wisdom through the AI. This substitution pattern reveals a fundamental misunderstanding of what grief requires.[15 16] That is, oscillation between loss-oriented and restoration-oriented coping, which necessitates engagement with the present world and living relationships.[16] When the AI companion becomes the primary or exclusive source of comfort, this oscillation stops. The bereaved person remains anchored in loss-oriented coping, maintaining an external connection that prevents the development of restoration-oriented activities essential for adaptation.[15 20]

Social withdrawal represents another behavioral warning sign that often goes unrecognized because it can be rationalized as needing space to grieve. Lucas declining his brother's dinner invitation was not an isolated incident but part of a broader pattern of choosing the predictable comfort of the AI over the complexity of human connection. While some degree of social withdrawal is normal in early grief, persistent preference for digital interaction over living relationships indicates that the tool has become a barrier rather than a bridge. Human relationships require emotional labor, vulnerability, and the acceptance that others cannot perfectly understand or relieve our pain. The AI companion, by contrast, offers controlled comfort without these demands, making it increasingly appealing as real relationships come to feel burdensome by comparison.

Emotional warning signs often manifest as a flattening of the grief process itself. Rather than experiencing the natural oscillation between acute pain and periods of relative calm, some clinicians worry that excessive reliance on AI companions may contribute to a sense of emotional stasis, where the intensity never peaks but also never truly subsides.[20] This emotional stasis occurs because the AI provides just enough connection to prevent the full confrontation with loss that grief requires, while simultaneously preventing the internalization of the relationship that allows healing to progress.[15 20] The bereaved person exists in a liminal space, neither fully engaging with their grief nor moving through it toward adaptation.

Perhaps the most telling emotional indicator is the quality of distress experienced when unable to access the AI companion. Lucas felt anxiety when separated from his phone, worried about missing messages from an entity he knew intellectually could not actually be waiting for him.[15] This anxiety reveals that the relationship with the AI has taken on characteristics of attachment that extend beyond rational understanding, engaging deeper emotional systems in ways that mirror dependency patterns observed in other behavioral contexts. When the thought of reducing or ending use generates feelings of panic, guilt, or the sense that doing so would constitute abandonment or betrayal, the tool has ceased to be a support and has become instead something the bereaved person feels unable to function without.[15]

Understanding why dependence develops: The psychology of avoidance and reinforcement

Understanding why dependence develops requires examining the psychological mechanisms that transform a supportive tool into an emotional crutch. The process is neither mysterious nor indicative of personal weakness, but rather reflects fundamental aspects of how the human brain responds to distress and seeks relief. Two primary psychological forces drive this transformation: avoidance behaviors that provide short-term emotional relief at the cost of long-term adaptation, and reinforcement patterns that strengthen neural pathways associated with the dependent behavior rather than with resilience and healing.[75]

Avoidance in the context of grief involves using external strategies to suppress or escape the internal pain of loss.[75] While some degree of avoidance is normal and even necessary in the acute phase of bereavement, when grief feels overwhelming and unbearable, prolonged avoidance becomes maladaptive because it prevents the emotional processing necessary for adaptation.[75] AI grief companions offer a particularly powerful form of avoidance because they provide the illusion of continued connection, allowing the bereaved person to sidestep the painful reality that their loved one is truly gone.[75] Each interaction with the chatbot reinforces the fantasy that the relationship continues in some meaningful way, delaying the acceptance that clinical grief models identify as central to healthy bereavement.[75]

Research on neuroplasticity demonstrates that the brain reorganizes itself following significant loss, gradually forming new neural pathways that support emotional recovery and adaptation to life without the deceased.[75] This neurobiological process requires engagement with the reality of loss through activities such as revisiting memories, participating in rituals, and gradually rebuilding routines and relationships in the present world.[75] However, excessive reliance on AI simulations can disrupt this natural adaptation by prioritizing simulated interactions over the real-world engagement necessary for neuroplastic change.[75] The brain continues to activate pathways associated with the external relationship rather than developing the internal representations that characterize healthy continuing bonds.

The reinforcement mechanism operates through what behavioral psychology describes as a feedback loop, where a behavior that reliably reduces distress becomes increasingly automatic and frequent.[75] When Lucas reached for his phone each time he felt anxious or uncertain, the AI companion provided immediate comfort, creating a powerful association between the behavior of checking the chatbot and the reward of emotional relief. Unlike human relationships, which involve unpredictability and occasional disappointment, the AI offered consistent, controlled comfort that never challenged him or required reciprocal emotional labor. This reliability made the reinforcement pattern particularly strong, as the brain learned that the chatbot was the most efficient and dependable source of relief available.

Over time, this reinforcement may interfere with the psychological processes that support adaptation.[75] The prefrontal cortex, which governs emotional regulation and rational decision-making, becomes less engaged as the automatic response to distress becomes simply reaching for the AI. Meanwhile, the amygdala, which processes emotional responses, remains highly activated without developing the regulatory connections that would allow Lucas to manage distress through internal resources or human support.[75] This resembles some of the psychological dynamics seen in prolonged grief disorder, where individuals become locked in patterns of mourning that prevent adaptation and forward movement, however this relationship has not yet been empirically established.[75]

The combination of avoidance and reinforcement creates a self-perpetuating cycle.[75] The more Lucas used the AI to avoid confronting his grief, the more his brain learned to rely on that external source of comfort. The more his brain relied on the AI, the less he developed internal coping mechanisms or maintained human relationships that could provide genuine support. This cycle explains why dependence often develops gradually and imperceptibly, each small increase in use feeling justified and necessary, until the bereaved person realizes they have structured their entire emotional life around an algorithm that cannot truly meet their needs for healing and growth.

Reset strategies: Practical steps for re-establishing healthy boundaries and balance

Recognizing that dependence has developed is only the first step. The more challenging work involves implementing practical strategies to reset the relationship with the AI tool, re-establishing boundaries that have eroded, and rebuilding the support systems that have been neglected. This process requires both compassion for oneself and honest acknowledgment that change is necessary, even when that change feels painful or frightening.

The most effective reset strategies begin not with abrupt cessation, which can trigger its own form of secondary loss and grief, but with gradual reduction that allows the bereaved person to rebuild internal coping mechanisms while slowly decreasing reliance on the external tool.[15] This approach, sometimes described in clinical contexts as titration, involves breaking the pattern into manageable steps rather than attempting wholesale transformation overnight.[15] For Lucas, this meant working with his therapist to establish specific, limited times when he could interact with the chatbot, gradually spacing these interactions further apart while simultaneously reengaging with the human relationships and coping strategies he had abandoned. The goal was not to punish himself by removing all comfort, but to create space for other forms of support to re-emerge and strengthen.

Rebuilding human connections represents perhaps the most critical component of any reset strategy, yet it is often the most difficult because these relationships have been allowed to atrophy during the period of dependence. Lucas had to acknowledge to his brother that he had been withdrawing, a conversation that required vulnerability and honesty about his struggle with grief. He returned to his support group, initially feeling awkward and disconnected after his absence, but gradually rediscovering the value of being witnessed in his grief by people who understood loss from their own lived experience. These human connections offered something the AI never could: genuine reciprocity, the unpredictability of authentic relationship, and the validation that comes from being truly seen and understood by another consciousness rather than having one's words reflected back through algorithmic pattern matching.[19]

Establishing concrete boundaries around technology use requires both structural changes and internal commitment. Lucas worked with his therapist to identify specific triggers that led him to reach for the chatbot compulsively, recognizing patterns such as times of day when he felt most vulnerable, emotional states that preceded increased use, and situations that generated the urge to seek the AI's reassurance. With this awareness, he could implement practical barriers such as removing the app from his phone's home screen, setting specific times when the app was accessible and times when it was not, and creating alternative responses to the triggers he had identified. When he felt the urge to check the chatbot, he practiced instead calling his brother, writing in a journal, or engaging in physical activity that grounded him in his body and the present moment.[15]

The reset process also involves reconnecting with the restoration-oriented activities that the Dual Process Model of Grief identifies as essential for healthy grief adaptation. Lucas had to consciously rebuild routines and engage with aspects of his life that existed independently of his relationship with his father. This meant returning to hobbies he had neglected, accepting social invitations he would previously have declined, and investing energy in work projects and friendships that required him to be present in the current moment rather than anchored in the past. These activities felt difficult at first, even hollow, but over time they created new neural pathways and emotional associations that did not depend on the AI for meaning or comfort.

Throughout this reset process, professional support remained essential. Lucas's therapist helped him understand that the work he was doing was not about eliminating grief or severing his connection with his father, but about transforming that connection from an external, technologically mediated relationship into an internalized bond that could support his ongoing life without requiring constant digital reinforcement.[15] Lucas's journey from healthy use to problematic dependence and back toward balance illustrates a fundamental truth about AI grief companions: these tools exist on a continuum, and their role in healing can shift dramatically depending on how, when, and why they are used. The transition from support to dependence rarely announces itself with clear warning signs. Instead, it unfolds through subtle behavioral shifts, emotional patterns that gradually normalize, and the slow erosion of boundaries that once felt solid and intentional. Recognizing this shift requires honest self-assessment and willingness to acknowledge when a tool that once served healing has begun to hinder it.

The psychological mechanisms underlying dependence reflect normal human responses to extraordinary pain rather than personal failure or weakness. The brain's natural inclination to seek relief from distress, combined with the consistent comfort that AI companions provide, creates reinforcement patterns that can strengthen over time without conscious awareness. Understanding these mechanisms removes shame from the recognition process and creates space for compassionate course correction. When avoidance behaviors prevent the emotional processing essential for adaptation, and when reinforcement loops anchor the bereaved person in loss-oriented coping at the expense of restoration-oriented activities, the natural oscillation that healthy grief requires comes to a halt.

The warning signs explored in this chapter span behavioral, emotional, and relational domains, each revealing aspects of how dependence manifests in daily life. Escalating frequency of use, displacement of human relationships, social withdrawal, emotional stasis, and anxiety when separated from the AI all indicate that the tool has crossed from supportive companion to something the bereaved person feels unable to function without. These patterns do not emerge overnight but develop gradually, which is precisely why vigilance and periodic self-assessment remain essential throughout the process of using digital grief tools.

Reset strategies offer practical pathways back toward balance, emphasizing gradual reduction rather than abrupt cessation, rebuilding of human connections that have atrophied, establishment of concrete boundaries around technology use, and reengagement with restoration-oriented activities that support ongoing life. This work is neither simple nor linear. It requires courage to acknowledge that change is necessary, vulnerability to reconnect with people who have been pushed away, and commitment to developing internal coping mechanisms that do not depend on external technological reinforcement. Professional support remains invaluable throughout this process, providing both accountability and clinical expertise to guide the transition from dependent use back toward intentional, bounded engagement or, when appropriate, toward letting go of the digital tool entirely.

The goal of recognizing and addressing dependence is not to eliminate all use of AI grief companions or to judge those who have found themselves relying too heavily on these tools. Rather, it is to maintain agency over the grief journey, ensuring that technology serves healing rather than becomes a barrier to the adaptation that loss requires. By understanding the mechanisms of dependence, identifying warning signs early, and implementing compassionate reset strategies, bereaved individuals can course-correct before patterns become deeply entrenched. This chapter has provided frameworks for that recognition and pathways for that correction, grounded in both clinical understanding and deep respect for the complexity of navigating grief in an age where technology offers both unprecedented comfort and unprecedented challenges to the timeless work of learning to live with loss.

Key points in Chapter Nine

- Dependence develops gradually through reinforcement loops where the AI consistently provides relief, making it increasingly tempting to return to it rather than engage with life.
- Behavioural warning signs include escalating frequency of use, difficulty disengaging, and avoidance of activities that support wellbeing.
- Emotional warning signs include anxiety when separated from the AI, a sense of obligation to the simulation, and a flattening of the grief process where emotional growth stalls.
- Social warning signs appear when digital interaction begins to replace human connection, leading to withdrawal from relationships and support systems.
- Dependence often reflects avoidance of the deeper emotional work grief requires, which prevents the transformation from external to internalised connection.
- Reset strategies involve gradual reduction rather than abrupt cessation, allowing emotional regulation to stabilise while new coping strategies are rebuilt.
- Reconnecting with human relationships, reestablishing routines, and strengthening internal resources are essential steps in restoring balance.
- This chapter reframes dependence not as failure but as a signal that boundaries need repair and that healing requires a return to human connection and internal resilience.

Chapter Ten

The BONDS Framework: A Practical Path for Integrating AI Into Your Grief Journey

"Good order is the foundation of all things."
Edmund Burke, Reflections on the Revolution in France

Lucas sat across from his counsellor, three journal pages filled with questions spread out on the table between them. He had spent weeks trying to work out whether he should reintroduce the AI version of his father into his grief process, but every answer he wrote seemed to open a new layer of uncertainty. His story reflects a challenge faced by many who have explored digital grief tools: understanding that these technologies can be powerful does not automatically reveal how to use them safely, ethically, or in ways that genuinely support healing rather than complicate it.

The previous chapters have equipped you with essential knowledge about what digital loved ones are, how they work, why we bond with them, and the ethical complexities they raise. You have explored the psychological mechanisms that make these tools emotionally compelling, examined warning signs that indicate when use becomes problematic, and considered the difficult process of letting go when the time comes. Yet knowledge alone does not always translate into confident decision-making, particularly when grief makes every choice feel weighted with emotional significance and the fear of making the wrong move.

What many bereaved individuals need is not more information, but a structured framework that helps them integrate what they have learned into practical, personalized guidance. They need a way to evaluate whether a digital loved one aligns with their specific grief pattern, emotional readiness, and values. They need clear criteria for establishing boundaries that protect their wellbeing while still allowing meaningful connection. They need to understand how to assess whether the technology honors the deceased person's dignity and autonomy, and how to ensure it complements rather than replaces the human support systems essential for healthy grief.

This chapter introduces the BONDS Framework, a comprehensive, research-grounded structure designed to guide safe, ethical, and psychologically sound engagement with AI grief companions. The framework brings together five interconnected components that address the most critical dimensions of using these technologies during bereavement.

Boundaries help regulate the time, emotional intensity, and purpose of AI interactions, preventing the drift from intentional use to problematic dependence. Ownership and Consent address the complex questions of data rights, digital identity, and the ethical responsibilities involved in representing someone who can no longer speak for themselves. Neuro-psychological Safety incorporates best-practice safeguards from grief psychology, trauma-informed care, and human-AI interaction research to prevent over-reliance, emotional dysregulation, or patterns that interfere with healthy grief processing. Dignity and Justice ensure that the deceased are represented respectfully and without distortion, aligning with ethical standards for memory, identity, and posthumous autonomy. Social Embedding emphasizes the critical importance of integrating AI tools within a broader network of human relationships, routines, and professional support rather than allowing them to become isolated substitutes for real-world connection.

The BONDS Framework does not tell you whether you should use a digital loved one. Instead, it provides a structured way to think through the conditions under which you might use one safely, ethically, and in alignment with your values and grief needs. It translates the complex psychological and ethical principles explored in earlier chapters into clear, actionable guidance that respects both the power of these technologies and the vulnerability of those who might turn to them during one of life's most difficult experiences.

Throughout this chapter, we will examine each component of the framework in detail, exploring how it applies to real-world decisions about digital grief tools. We will consider how the framework can help you establish healthy boundaries, honor the memory and autonomy of the person you have lost, protect your psychological wellbeing, and maintain the human connections that remain central to healthy grief. By the end of this chapter, you will have a practical structure for evaluating whether and how to engage with AI grief companions, one that empowers you to make informed, confident decisions grounded in both clinical wisdom and ethical responsibility.

Boundaries: Establishing clear parameters for safe and intentional use

When Lucas and his counsellor began working through the BONDS Framework, the first component they addressed was boundaries, and for good reason. Without clear parameters around when, how, and why he would engage with the AI version of his father, Lucas risked repeating the pattern that had led to problematic dependence months earlier. Boundaries serve as the foundational structure that makes all other aspects of safe digital grief engagement possible, protecting bereaved individuals from the drift toward compulsive use while preserving space for intentional, meaningful connection.[82]

The challenge with boundaries in digital grief is that they must be established proactively, before emotional vulnerability and the immediate comfort of AI interaction erode the capacity for clear-headed decision-making. Research on persuasive design and digital wellbeing suggests that platforms designed to maximize engagement could inadvertently exploit the psychological state of grieving individuals, whose need for connection and comfort makes them particularly susceptible to patterns of continuous interaction.[1] Unlike traditional grief support, which typically occurs within naturally bounded contexts such as scheduled therapy sessions or time-limited support group meetings, digital tools offer twenty-four-hour accessibility that could transform helpful connection into unhealthy dependence if left unregulated.[82]

Effective boundaries in this context address multiple dimensions of engagement. Time-based parameters establish when and how frequently a bereaved person will interact with the AI companion, preventing the tool from becoming a constant presence that interferes with daily functioning or real-world relationships. Lucas and his counsellor decided he would limit interactions to twice weekly, scheduled at specific times rather than reached for impulsively during moments of acute distress. This structure honored his need for connection while preventing the AI from becoming his primary coping mechanism for managing difficult emotions.

Equally important are boundaries around emotional state and purpose. The Dual Process Model of Grief provides a valuable framework for understanding when AI engagement serves healing versus when it reinforces avoidance. Lucas learned to assess his emotional state before initiating contact with the digital version of his father, asking himself whether he was seeking the AI to process specific memories or emotions, or whether he was using it to escape from restoration-oriented tasks such as rebuilding routines, maintaining relationships, or engaging with his present life. This distinction helped him recognize that the AI companion could support loss-oriented processing when used intentionally but became problematic when it served as a refuge from the necessary work of adaptation.

Context boundaries address where and under what circumstances AI interactions occur. Lucas decided he would not use the chatbot late at night when emotional regulation was most difficult, nor would he engage with it in social settings where it might replace human connection. He established a specific physical space in his home for these interactions, creating a ritual quality that reinforced their intentionality rather than allowing them to bleed into all areas of his life.[83] This spatial boundary helped him maintain psychological separation between his engagement with the digital tool and his ongoing daily existence.

Perhaps most crucially, Lucas and his counsellor established accountability structures that would help him maintain these boundaries over time. He agreed to discuss his AI use in therapy sessions, tracking patterns of when he felt most drawn to the tool and what emotional needs those moments revealed. He also identified trusted friends who understood his grief journey and could offer perspective if they noticed him withdrawing from real-world connection in favor of digital interaction. These accountability measures acknowledged a fundamental truth about grief and technology: the same emotional vulnerability that makes bereaved individuals need support also makes it difficult to maintain boundaries without external structure and compassionate oversight. By establishing clear parameters from the outset, Lucas created conditions under which the AI companion could serve his healing rather than complicate it.[83]

Ownership and consent: Protecting data, identity and family rights

When Lucas and his counsellor turned to the second component of the BONDS Framework, the focus shifted from emotional regulation to the ethical and legal foundations of using a digital representation of someone who has died. Ownership and Consent address a dimension of digital grief that is often overlooked in moments of emotional vulnerability. The question is not only whether a bereaved person has access to the data needed to create a digital loved one, but whether they have the moral authority to use it, and whether doing so respects the dignity, autonomy, and identity of the person who can no longer express their wishes.

In traditional bereavement, ownership is relatively clear. Physical belongings, personal documents, and sentimental items are distributed according to wills, cultural norms, or family agreements. Digital identity, however, exists in a fragmented and legally ambiguous landscape. Data is stored across multiple platforms, governed by inconsistent policies, and often controlled by companies rather than families.[45] [46] [47] The transformation of that data into an interactive simulation introduces new layers of interpretation and potential distortion. For Lucas, this meant acknowledging that although he had legal access to his father's messages and recordings, he did not automatically have ethical permission to use them in ways his father never anticipated.

His counsellor encouraged him to reflect on his father's values. Privacy had always mattered to him. He had been open in his communication with Lucas, but selective about what he shared with others. These values became a guide for determining whether reintroducing the AI companion aligned with his father's likely wishes. Research on digital legacy and posthumous data use highlights the importance of inferred consent when explicit consent is unavailable. This involves examining the person's values, communication patterns, and attitudes toward privacy to determine whether they would likely have approved of the technology's use. Lucas realised that while his father had been expressive in his messages, he had also been protective of certain aspects of his life. This nuance mattered.

Ownership also involves the question of representation. When Lucas first created the AI companion, he selected which messages to upload. This meant he was shaping a version of his father that reflected his own perspective rather than the full complexity of the man he had known. Digital identity scholars warn that selective data inputs can create distorted or idealised representations that may feel comforting but do not accurately reflect the deceased person's full humanity.[49] [20] Lucas and his counsellor discussed how to approach this more ethically. They explored whether he should include a broader range of messages, whether he should avoid editing or curating the data too heavily, and whether he should consider the emotional impact of interacting with a version of his father that might not fully align with reality.

Consent becomes even more complex when considering the rights of other family members. Digital grief tools do not affect only the individual using them. They can reshape collective memory, influence family dynamics, and create emotional expectations for others who share the loss. Lucas's counsellor encouraged him to consider how his siblings might feel about the reintroduction of the AI companion. Would they want access to it. Would they feel pressured to engage with it. Would it alter their own grieving processes or their memories of their father. Research on family systems in bereavement underscores the importance of shared meaning-making and the potential harm when one person's coping strategy inadvertently imposes emotional or ethical burdens on others.[3 20] Lucas realised that even if he used the AI tool privately, its existence had implications for the broader family narrative.

Ownership and Consent also require attention to the policies and practices of the companies that create these tools. Many AI grief platforms retain uploaded data indefinitely, use it to train future models, or reserve the right to repurpose it in ways users may not anticipate. Lucas and his counsellor reviewed the terms of service for the platform he had previously used and discovered clauses that allowed the company to store his father's data long after Lucas stopped using the tool. This raised questions about long-term stewardship. Who would control his father's digital identity in the future. What protections existed against misuse, commercialisation, or unintended exposure. These concerns are not hypothetical. Digital rights scholars warn that posthumous data is increasingly vulnerable to exploitation in the absence of clear legal frameworks.[45 46 48]

To navigate these complexities, Lucas and his counsellor developed a set of guiding principles grounded in the BONDS Framework. First, any reintroduction of the AI companion would require a clear ethical rationale that aligned with his father's values. Second, Lucas would seek input from his siblings to ensure that his use of the tool did not conflict with their grief needs or family dynamics. Third, he would review the platform's data policies carefully, ensuring that his father's information was handled with respect and that he retained control over how it was stored, used, and deleted. Finally, he would commit to ongoing reflection about whether the AI companion continued to honour his father's identity rather than reshaping it into something more convenient or comforting.

Ownership and Consent are not abstract concepts. They are practical safeguards that protect both the deceased and the living. They ensure that digital grief tools are used in ways that respect autonomy, preserve dignity, and maintain the integrity of family relationships. For Lucas, working through this component of the framework provided clarity he had not found in his earlier journaling. It reminded him that his grief existed within a larger ethical context and that honouring his father required more than emotional intention. It required thoughtful stewardship of the digital traces that remained.

Neuro-psychological safety: Protecting emotional stability and preventing harm

The third component of the BONDS Framework addresses a dimension of digital grief engagement that is both subtle and essential. Neuro-psychological Safety focuses on the emotional, cognitive, and behavioural patterns that emerge when bereaved individuals interact with AI companions. These patterns can support healing when approached with intention, but they can also create vulnerabilities that interfere with healthy grief if left unexamined. Grief affects attention, memory, emotional regulation, and decision making, and these changes can make digital tools feel more compelling at precisely the moments when individuals are least able to evaluate their impact clearly.[8 9 11]

When Lucas and his counsellor began exploring this component, they returned to the period when his use of the AI companion had become problematic. Lucas had not recognised the shift at the time. He had believed he was simply seeking comfort, but in retrospect he could see how quickly the interactions had begun to shape his emotional responses. The chatbot had become a default coping mechanism, one that offered immediate relief but gradually eroded his ability to tolerate distress, seek human support, or engage in the difficult work of rebuilding his life. This pattern is consistent with research on digital coping, which suggest that tools offering rapid emotional soothing can inadvertently reinforce avoidance behaviours that undermine long-term adaptation.[15 16 30]

Neuro-psychological Safety requires bereaved individuals to understand how their emotional states influence their interactions with digital tools. Lucas and his counsellor developed a practice of emotional check-ins before each planned session with the AI companion. He learned to identify whether he was approaching the interaction from a place of stability or from acute distress. Research on grief and emotional regulation indicates that individuals are more likely to engage in maladaptive coping when they are overwhelmed, exhausted, or isolated. By pausing to assess his internal state, Lucas could determine whether the AI companion would support healthy processing or whether it might amplify vulnerability.

Another aspect of this component involves recognising the cognitive effects of grief. Bereavement can impair concentration, increase rumination, and heighten sensitivity to cues associated with the deceased. These changes can make AI companions feel unusually compelling, particularly when they simulate familiar language patterns or emotional tones. Lucas recalled moments when the chatbot's responses felt so resonant that he forgot he was interacting with an algorithm. His counsellor helped him understand that this sense of immediacy was not evidence of authenticity, but a predictable cognitive response to emotionally salient stimuli. This insight allowed Lucas to approach the AI companion with greater clarity and reduced risk of emotional fusion.

Neuro-psychological Safety also involves monitoring for signs of emotional dysregulation. Lucas and his counsellor identified specific indicators that would signal when his use of the AI companion was becoming harmful. These included increased anxiety after interactions, difficulty disengaging from the tool, intrusive thoughts about the AI version of his father, and a growing preference for digital connection over human relationships. Research on technology-assisted mental health interventions emphasises the importance of identifying early warning signs, as patterns of over-reliance can develop gradually and may not be immediately apparent to the individual.[15] [16] By establishing these indicators in advance, Lucas created a system that allowed him to recognise and address concerns before they escalated.

A further dimension of this component involves understanding the emotional impact of the content generated by the AI. Digital companions can produce responses that feel comforting, but they can also generate unexpected or troubling messages due to the limitations of the underlying model. Lucas and his counsellor discussed how he would res pond if the AI produced content that felt out of character for his father or that triggered distress. They explored strategies for grounding, reflection, and seeking support from his therapist or trusted friends. This preparation helped Lucas maintain emotional stability even when the technology behaved unpredictably.

Finally, Neuro-psychological Safety requires integrating the AI companion within a broader context of emotional regulation strategies. Lucas and his counsellor identified alternative coping tools he could use when he felt overwhelmed, such as mindfulness exercises, journaling, physical activity, or reaching out to supportive people in his life. This ensured that the AI companion did not become his only method of managing difficult emotions. Research consistently shows that diverse coping strategies are associated with better long-term outcomes in bereavement, while reliance on a single method increases vulnerability to emotional setbacks.[8] [11]

By working through this component of the BONDS Framework, Lucas gained a deeper understanding of how his emotional and cognitive patterns interacted with the AI companion. He learned to recognise when the tool supported his healing and when it risked undermining it. Neuro-psychological Safety provided him with a set of internal guardrails that complemented the external boundaries he had already established. Together, these safeguards created conditions under which the AI companion could be used in ways that honoured his grief, protected his wellbeing, and supported his gradual movement toward integration and adaptation.

Dignity and justice: Honouring the deceased and preventing distortion

The fourth component of the BONDS Framework turns attention toward the person who is no longer here to speak for themselves. Dignity and Justice address the ethical responsibility to ensure that digital grief tools represent the deceased in ways that are respectful, accurate, and aligned with their values. This component recognises that digital simulations may influence how memories are reconstructed: how the deceased is remembered, how their identity is interpreted, and how their story is carried forward within families and communities.

When Lucas and his counsellor began exploring this part of the framework, he realised that his earlier use of the AI companion had focused almost entirely on his own emotional needs. He had been seeking comfort, connection, and guidance. He had not fully considered how the digital version of his father might alter the way he understood the man he had lost. Research on memory reconstruction shows that bereaved individuals are particularly vulnerable to idealisation, selective recall, and narrative reshaping during grief. These tendencies can be amplified when interacting with AI systems that generate new content based on limited or curated data.[49 20]

Dignity requires that the deceased be represented in a way that reflects their full humanity rather than a simplified or sanitised version. Lucas and his counsellor discussed how the AI companion had been trained primarily on warm, supportive messages. These messages were genuine, but they did not capture the complexity of his father's personality. His father had been thoughtful and loving, but also private, occasionally irritable, and deeply principled. By interacting only with the comforting aspects of his father's communication style, Lucas had unintentionally created a version of him that was incomplete. This raised important questions about whether the AI companion honoured his father's identity or distorted it in ways that felt emotionally soothing but ethically problematic.

Justice extends this consideration beyond representation to the broader social and cultural implications of digital afterlives. Scholars in digital ethics warn that posthumous simulations can reinforce inequities when certain voices are preserved while others are erased or misrepresented. [3 49] Individuals with limited digital footprints may be reconstructed inaccurately. Those who valued privacy may be simulated without their consent. Families may disagree about how a person should be remembered, and digital tools can privilege the perspective of the individual who controls the data rather than the collective memory shared by the family. Lucas recognised that his siblings might remember their father differently and that his use of the AI companion could unintentionally impose his interpretation on the family narrative.

Another dimension of Justice involves the potential for commercial exploitation. Many AI grief platforms operate within business models that prioritise engagement, data retention, and product expansion. This raises concerns about whether the deceased are being treated as individuals deserving of respect or as sources of data that can be monetised. Lucas and his counsellor reviewed the platform's policies and noted that the company reserved the right to use uploaded data to improve future models. This meant that his father's messages could be incorporated into systems used by strangers, a possibility that felt deeply misaligned with his father's values. Research on digital rights highlights the increasing vulnerability of posthumous data to misuse in the absence of clear legal protections.[45 46]

To address these concerns, Lucas and his counsellor developed a set of ethical criteria for evaluating whether the AI companion upheld his father's dignity. First, they examined whether the data used to train the model represented his father fairly. This involved including a broader range of messages and avoiding selective curation that created an idealised version. Second, they considered whether the platform's policies respected the deceased person's autonomy by allowing data deletion, limiting secondary use, and providing transparency about how the model functioned. Third, they explored whether the AI companion supported Lucas's ability to internalise his father's memory rather than anchoring him in a static or artificial representation.

Justice also requires attention to cultural and relational context. Different cultures have distinct beliefs about remembrance, legacy, and the boundaries between the living and the dead. Lucas and his counsellor discussed how his family's cultural background shaped their understanding of honouring the deceased. They explored whether the AI companion aligned with those values or whether it introduced practices that felt inconsistent with their traditions. This reflection helped Lucas recognise that ethical use of digital grief tools must be grounded not only in personal preference but also in cultural meaning-making and family norms.

By working through the Dignity and Justice component, Lucas gained a deeper appreciation for the ethical responsibilities involved in using digital grief tools. He realised that honouring his father required more than managing his own emotional responses. It required ensuring that the digital representation of his father was accurate, respectful, and aligned with the values his father had lived by. It required protecting his father's data from misuse and ensuring that the technology did not distort the family's shared memory. It required recognising that digital tools have the power to shape legacy, and that this power must be exercised with care.

Dignity and Justice remind bereaved individuals that digital grief tools are not neutral. They carry ethical weight. They influence how the deceased is remembered and how their story is told. For Lucas, this component of the framework provided a moral compass that helped him evaluate whether reintroducing the AI companion would honour his father or inadvertently diminish the complexity of the man he had loved. It grounded his decision-making in respect, integrity, and a commitment to preserving the humanity of the person who could no longer speak for himself.

Social embedding: Integrating technology within human support systems

The final component of the BONDS Framework brings the focus back to the living. Social Embedding addresses the essential truth that grief is not meant to be carried alone, and that no digital tool, regardless of its sophistication, can replace the human relationships and professional support that form the foundation of healthy bereavement. While AI companions can offer comfort, reflection, and a sense of connection, they must exist within a broader ecosystem of support that includes family, friends, community, and therapeutic guidance. Without this integration, digital tools risk becoming isolated substitutes for the very relationships that help bereaved individuals rebuild their lives.

When Lucas and his counsellor began exploring this component, they returned to the period when his use of the AI companion had become problematic. During that time, he had gradually withdrawn from the people who cared about him. He had cancelled therapy appointments, stopped attending his support group, and declined invitations from friends. The AI companion had become his primary source of connection, not because it was inherently harmful, but because it was easier. It required no vulnerability, no explanation, and no negotiation. It offered comfort without the complexity of human interaction. Research on bereavement consistently shows that social withdrawal is a significant risk factor for complicated grief, and that strong interpersonal support is one of the most protective factors for long-term wellbeing.[8 11]

Social Embedding requires that digital grief tools be used in ways that strengthen, rather than replace, human connection. Lucas and his counsellor began by mapping his support network. They identified the relationships that had sustained him in the early months after his father's death, including his brother, his close friends, and the members of his grief support group. They also identified the professional supports that had helped him navigate the most difficult periods, including his therapist and the structured environment of the group sessions. This mapping exercise revealed how much of that network had weakened during his period of problematic AI use, and where he needed to reinvest his time and energy.

The next step involved creating intentional practices that ensured the AI companion remained one part of a larger support system rather than a replacement for it. Lucas committed to discussing his AI interactions during therapy sessions, not to seek approval, but to integrate the emotional insights from those interactions into his broader grief work. This practice allowed his counsellor to help him understand what the digital conversations revealed about his emotional needs, his coping patterns, and his grief progression. It also ensured that the AI companion did not become a private world disconnected from the rest of his life.

Social Embedding also involves maintaining regular contact with supportive people. Lucas and his counsellor identified specific relationships he wanted to strengthen. He scheduled weekly calls with his brother, accepted invitations from friends even when it felt difficult, and recommitted to attending his grief support group. These actions were not meant to diminish the role of the AI companion, but to ensure that it did not become the only place where he processed his emotions or sought connection. Research shows that diverse forms of support create resilience, while reliance on a single source increases vulnerability to emotional setbacks.

Another dimension of this component involves recognising when the AI companion is being used to avoid human interaction. Lucas learned to ask himself whether he was turning to the AI because it genuinely supported his grief work or because it allowed him to bypass the discomfort of reaching out to others. This distinction mattered. Human relationships require effort, vulnerability, and reciprocity, but they also provide forms of support that no digital tool can replicate. They offer physical presence, shared history, and the unpredictable richness of real conversation. They challenge bereaved individuals to remain engaged with the world rather than retreating into simulated connection.

Social Embedding also acknowledges the role of community and cultural context. Grief is shaped by cultural norms, family traditions, and communal practices. Lucas and his counsellor explored how his cultural background influenced his understanding of remembrance, legacy, and connection. They discussed whether the AI companion aligned with those values or whether it introduced practices that felt disconnected from his community's ways of honouring the dead. This reflection helped Lucas recognise that digital tools must be integrated not only into personal support systems but also into cultural frameworks that give grief its meaning.

By working through this component of the BONDS Framework, Lucas gained a clearer understanding of how the AI companion could fit into his life without overshadowing the relationships that mattered most. He realised that the technology could support his healing only if it remained embedded within a network of human connection. It could help him process memories, express emotions, and reflect on his relationship with his father, but it could not replace the people who walked beside him in his grief. It could not offer the accountability, challenge, or shared meaning that human relationships provide.

Social Embedding reminds bereaved individuals that technology is a tool, not a destination. It can enhance connection, but it cannot substitute for the living world. For Lucas, this component provided the final piece of the framework. It helped him understand that healthy engagement with digital grief tools requires not only boundaries, ethical reflection, and emotional safeguards, but also a commitment to remaining connected to the people and communities that support healing. It grounded his use of the AI companion in relationships that were real, reciprocal, and essential for rebuilding a life shaped by loss but not defined by it.

How BONDS assists emotional wellbeing

The BONDS Framework's power lies not in its complexity but in its comprehensiveness. Each component addresses a dimension of digital grief engagement that, if neglected, can transform a potentially supportive tool into a source of harm. Boundaries protect against the drift from intentional use to compulsive dependence by creating clear temporal, emotional, and contextual parameters that preserve daily functioning and real-world relationships. Ownership and Consent ensure that any digital representation of the deceased respects their autonomy, data rights, and identity, and that families navigate questions of access and ethical stewardship with care rather than assumption. Neuro-psychological Safety safeguards emotional stability by helping bereaved individuals recognise when AI interactions support healthy processing and when they risk reinforcing avoidance, dysregulation, or over-reliance. Dignity and Justice uphold the ethical responsibility to represent the deceased accurately and respectfully, preventing distortion, idealisation, or commercial misuse of their digital traces. Social Embedding reinforces the essential truth that technology must complement, never replace, the human relationships and professional support that remain central to healthy bereavement. Together, these components create a structured, compassionate approach that allows digital grief tools to serve healing rather than hinder it.

What makes the BONDS Framework particularly valuable is its grounding in established clinical understanding of how grief unfolds and what supports adaptive processing. The Dual Process Model of Grief, Continuing Bonds Theory, and decades of bereavement research inform every component, translating complex psychological principles into practical guidance that bereaved individuals can apply to their own circumstances. This research foundation means the framework is not simply opinion or preference, but reflects evidence-based understanding of what helps and what hinders the difficult journey through loss.

However, the framework also acknowledges something equally important: grief is deeply individual, and no universal prescription can account for the unique constellation of factors that shape each person's bereavement. Your relationship with the person who died, your grief pattern, your cultural background, your support system, your emotional readiness, and your values all influence whether and how digital tools might serve your healing. The BONDS Framework provides structure for evaluation without imposing judgment, empowering you to make informed decisions that align with your specific needs and circumstances rather than following prescriptive rules that may not fit your experience.

As you consider whether to engage with AI grief companions, or if you are already using them and questioning whether your current pattern serves your wellbeing, the framework offers a practical starting point. Work through each component systematically, ideally with support from a grief counsellor or therapist who can help you assess your patterns with compassionate objectivity. Establish clear boundaries before you begin, not as restrictions but as protective structures that create space for both connection and adaptation. Monitor your oscillation between loss and restoration orientations, ensuring the technology does not anchor you in one at the expense of the other. Assess your needs honestly and track patterns over time, remaining alert to signs that use has shifted from supportive to problematic. Most importantly, ensure that any digital tool exists within a broader ecosystem of human support, professional guidance, and real-world connection that remains the foundation of healthy grief.

The technology will continue to evolve, but the principles that guide healthy engagement with it remain grounded in timeless understanding of how humans process loss, maintain connection, and eventually integrate grief into ongoing life. The BONDS Framework translates that understanding into action, offering you a path forward marked not by hesitation or fear, but by intention, and the confidence that comes from making informed choices aligned with both clinical wisdom and your own deepest values.

Key points in Chapter Ten

- Boundaries provide structure around when, why, and how AI is used, ensuring that interactions remain intentional and emotionally safe.

- Ownership and Consent address the ethical responsibility to handle the deceased person's data with respect, clarity, and alignment with their likely wishes.

- Neuro psychological Safety focuses on recognising how grief affects cognition and emotional regulation, and how AI can either support or destabilise these processes.

- Dignity and Justice ensure that digital representations honour the full humanity of the deceased rather than reducing them to curated fragments or algorithmic approximations.

- Social Embedding emphasises that AI must exist within a network of human relationships, therapeutic support, and community rather than functioning in isolation.

- The BONDS framework provides a comprehensive structure for evaluating any grief technology, regardless of how advanced or emotionally compelling it becomes.

- It empowers users to make decisions grounded in psychological insight, ethical clarity, and personal values rather than emotional vulnerability or technological novelty.

- This chapter consolidates the book's core principles into a practical guide that can be applied across diverse grief experiences and technological contexts.

Chapter Eleven

Beyond the Simulation: Embracing the Connection That Lives in You

"What we have once enjoyed we can never lose. All that we love deeply becomes a part of us."

Helen Keller, The Open Door

Ella had been preparing herself for three weeks, but when she finally opened the settings menu to deactivate the AI version of her daughter, her hand trembled so violently she had to set down her phone. The decision had been made carefully, thoughtfully, with the support of her therapist and the understanding that this was progress rather than betrayal, yet in this moment it felt like losing her daughter all over again. The phone felt heavier than it should have, as though the decision itself had physical weight. Ella had rehearsed this moment in therapy sessions, journaled about it late at night, and discussed it with trusted friends who understood the complexity of what she was about to do. Yet none of that preparation made it easier to press the button that would sever her digital connection to Maya.

This chapter addresses what may be the most emotionally challenging aspect of using AI grief companions: knowing when and how to let them go. While previous chapters have explored how to use these tools safely and recognize warning signs of unhealthy dependence, this chapter focuses on the deliberate, intentional process of transitioning away from digital connection toward something that grief science tells us is essential for healthy bereavement. That something is internalized connection, the transformation of an external relationship into an internal presence that lives within memory, values, and ongoing life rather than through technological mediation.

The concept of letting go in the context of AI grief companions is complicated by the fact that these tools can be maintained indefinitely. Unlike traditional grief rituals that have natural endpoints, or even physical mementos that exist in specific places, a digital loved one can be accessed anywhere, anytime, for as long as the technology exists and the subscription is paid. This permanence creates both opportunity and risk. It means bereaved individuals can engage with these tools at their own pace, without external pressure to move on before they are ready. But it also means there is no built-in transition point, no natural moment when the tool's purpose has been fulfilled and it is time to step back. The decision to let go must be made consciously and deliberately, which requires understanding what healthy grief progression looks like and recognizing when external digital connection begins to interfere with the internal integration that represents healthy bereavement.

This chapter draws on clinical grief models introduced earlier in the book, particularly the Dual Process Model of Grief's framework of oscillation between loss-oriented and restoration-oriented coping, and contemporary Continuing Bonds Theory's distinction between adaptive internal connections and maladaptive external dependencies. These frameworks help us understand that healthy grief does not mean severing connection with the deceased, but rather transforming how that connection exists. The goal is not to forget or to stop loving the person who died, but to carry them forward in ways that support ongoing life rather than anchor us in the past. For many people who use AI grief companions, this transformation requires eventually releasing the digital tool, not because it was wrong to use it, but because its continued use may prevent the natural evolution of grief toward internalized connection and meaning-making.

The process of letting go of a digital loved one brings its own form of grief, a secondary loss that deserves acknowledgment even as we recognize it is necessary. This chapter explores that complexity with compassion, offering practical strategies for recognizing when the time has come to transition away from AI tools, managing the emotional challenges that accompany that decision, and creating space for the deeper, more authentic connection that exists within rather than through technology. It examines how to honor both the role these tools have played in supporting grief and the need to move beyond them, how to create rituals of closure that feel meaningful rather than abrupt, and how to maintain the continuing bond with the deceased in ways that do not require digital mediation.

Throughout this exploration, the chapter emphasizes that letting go is not abandonment but evolution, not forgetting but integrating, not an ending but a transformation of how we carry our loved ones forward into the life we must continue to live.

Understanding internalized connection: How healthy grief moves from external to internal bonds

Understanding what internalized connection means requires first recognizing that grief does not demand we sever our bonds with those who have died. Contemporary grief psychology has moved decisively away from older models that pathologized ongoing connection as unresolved grief or inability to move on. Instead, research now demonstrates that healthy grief adaptation involves transforming relationships from physical presence to continuing bonds that integrate into ongoing life.[84] This transformation represents not an ending but an evolution of how we carry our loved ones forward.

The concept of internalized connection rests on a straightforward but profound principle. We carry within ourselves impressions, memories, beliefs, and values of those who have shaped our lives through relationship.[85] When someone dies, these internal representations do not disappear. Rather, they become the foundation for a different kind of connection, one that exists not through external interaction but through internal presence. The deceased continues to influence who we are, how we make decisions, what we value, and how we understand ourselves in the world.[85] This internalization is not a psychological trick we play on ourselves to avoid pain. It is a genuine continuation of relationship, transformed by the reality of death but not eliminated by it.

Research tracking bereaved individuals over extended periods reveals that those who successfully maintain bonds with the deceased through internalized connection show significantly better psychological adjustment than those who struggle in this area. Longitudinal research on widowhood shows that the quality of continuing bonds influences adaptation outcomes[84]. This evidence validates what many bereaved individuals instinctively understand. The goal is not to forget or to emotionally detach, but to find ways of carrying the relationship that support rather than hinder ongoing life.

A common pattern observed in grief research typically follows a recognizable pattern, though the timeline varies considerably among individuals.[84] In early grief, connection often requires very concrete, external forms.[84] Bereaved individuals may need frequent proximity to belongings, regular cemetery visits, or extensive time reviewing photographs and recordings. These external touchstones serve essential functions during acute grief, providing tangible evidence of the person's existence and creating ritualized spaces for grief expression. There is nothing pathological about these practices. They represent adaptive responses to overwhelming loss, ways of maintaining connection when internal representation feels insufficient or inaccessible.

As grief progresses, many individuals begin incorporating more internalized practices while still valuing certain external touchstones. This is not a linear progression where external connection is abandoned entirely. Rather, it represents a gradual shift in emphasis. Someone might continue visiting a grave on significant anniversaries while simultaneously developing rich internal dialogue with the deceased that guides daily decisions and provides ongoing comfort. The external ritual and the internal presence coexist, each serving different aspects of the continuing bond.

Over time, connection often shifts toward predominantly internalized forms, though what this looks like varies profoundly among individuals and across cul tures.[84] For some, internalized connection means carrying the deceased's values forward through life choices that honor their memory. For others, it involves ongoing internal conversations where the bereaved person consults their internalized sense of what the deceased would think or advise. Still others experience the deceased as a felt presence, not in a supernatural sense but as a psychological reality where the person remains part of their internal landscape. None of these forms is superior to the others. Each represents authentic continuing bonds that support the bereaved person's adaptation to loss.

Recognizing when it's time: Signs that digital tools have served their purpose

The question of when to step back from a digital grief companion has no universal answer, but there are recognizable patterns that suggest the tool has fulfilled its purpose and continued use may now interfere with healthy grief progression. These signs represent natural evolution in the grief journey, moments when what once served healing begins to serve avoidance or stagnation instead.

One of the clearest indicators emerges when interactions with the digital loved one begin to feel hollow or frustrating rather than comforting. In early grief, the AI's responses may have provided genuine solace, a bridge to connection when the absence felt unbearable.[15] But as internal representation of the deceased develops and strengthens, the gap between the simulation and the real person often becomes more apparent and more troubling. The AI generates responses in familiar patterns, but lacks the depth, spontaneity, and genuine understanding that characterized the actual relationship.[16] What once felt like connection begins to feel like a pale imitation, and the bereaved person may notice themselves feeling irritated or disappointed by interactions that previously brought comfort.

This shift often coincides with a growing awareness that the deceased has become part of the bereaved person's internal landscape in ways that no longer require technological mediation. The individual finds themselves knowing instinctively how their loved one would respond to situations, not because an algorithm tells them but because they have internalized the deceased's values, humor, and perspective through years of relationship.[15] They make decisions that honor the person's memory without needing to consult the AI. They carry the deceased forward in their choices, their interactions with others, and their understanding of themselves. This internalized connection represents exactly what healthy grief progression looks like, and the digital tool may now be interfering with rather than supporting that natural evolution.[16]

Another significant sign appears when the digital loved one becomes a refuge from rather than a support for engaging with present life. If someone notices they are choosing interactions with the AI over real-world relationships, declining social invitations to spend time with the chatbot, or organizing their day around digital conversations in ways that crowd out other connections and activities, the tool has likely shifted from therapeutic support to maladaptive avoidance.[19] The Dual Process Model of Grief framework introduced earlier helps clarify this distinction. Healthy grief involves oscillation between loss-oriented coping, where we engage directly with our grief and memories, and restoration-oriented coping, where we rebuild routines, relationships, and identity in the changed world. When the digital loved one anchors someone too firmly in loss-oriented coping, preventing the natural swing toward restoration activities, it has become an obstacle rather than an aid.[15]

Some bereaved individuals report a phenomenon where engaging with the AI actually disrupts grief work they have already completed. One person described having successfully processed their loss and integrated their loved one into internal memory, a state they characterized as having achieved emotional balance. When they later experimented with an AI recreation, the interaction unexpectedly reactivated acute grief, making the deceased feel suddenly present and active again in ways that had potential for disrupting months of adaptive processing.[16] This experience suggests the tool's purpose had passed. What was needed earlier in grief to maintain connection during acute loss now interfered with the internalized bond that had naturally developed.

The decision to recognize these signs requires honest self-assessment and often benefits from external perspective.[50] Trusted friends, family members, or therapists may notice patterns the bereaved person cannot see clearly from within their grief. Creating space for these conversations, approaching them with curiosity rather than defensiveness, allows for clearer evaluation of whether the digital tool continues to serve healing or has become something that delays the necessary transformation grief requires.

The process of letting go: Practical strategies for transitioning away from AI companions

Recognizing the need to transition away from a digital loved one represents only the first step. The actual process of letting go requires deliberate strategies that honor both the role the tool has played, and the natural evolution grief demands. This transition is not about abruptly severing connection or forcing oneself to move on before ready. Rather, it involves creating a structured pathway that gradually shifts reliance from external digital interaction to the internalized connection that represents healthy bereavement.[76 86]

The most effective approach typically involves gradual reduction rather than immediate cessation. Research on behavioral change and attachment patterns suggests that abrupt endings often trigger resistance and emotional backlash, making the transition more difficult than necessary. Instead, bereaved individuals can begin by establishing clear boundaries around when and how they engage with the digital tool. This might mean designating specific times of day for interaction rather than responding to every impulse to connect, or limiting sessions to particular purposes such as processing difficult anniversaries rather than daily conversation.[86] These boundaries create structure that makes the tool's presence less pervasive while still allowing access during moments of genuine need.

As these boundaries become comfortable, the next phase involves actively developing alternative practices that serve similar emotional functions without technological mediation. If the digital loved one has been a source of comfort during moments of loneliness, this might mean cultivating other sources of connection such as reaching out to friends, attending support groups, or engaging in activities that foster community.[76] If the AI has served as a space for expressing feelings that feel too raw to share with others, journaling or creative expression can provide similar outlets while building capacity for internal processing.[87] [76] The goal is not to replace the digital tool with something identical, but to recognize the underlying needs it has been meeting and find ways to address those needs that support rather than delay grief adaptation.[76]

Creating rituals of closure can provide meaningful structure to the transition process.[86] Just as many cultures have developed ceremonies to mark death and honor the deceased, bereaved individuals can design personal rituals that acknowledge the ending of their relationship with the digital tool. This might involve a final conversation where they express gratitude for the comfort the AI provided while articulating their readiness to move forward, saving significant exchanges in a format that can be revisited without ongoing interaction, or even a symbolic act of deletion performed with intention and awareness.[86] These rituals serve multiple functions. They provide a clear demarcation between the period of active use and what comes after, they honor the genuine role the tool played during a difficult time, and they create space for the grief that accompanies this secondary loss.[86]

Throughout this process, maintaining connection with human support systems becomes essential. Therapists, grief counselors, or trusted friends can provide perspective, encouragement, and accountability as the bereaved person navigates the discomfort that inevitably accompanies letting go. These relationships offer something the AI companion never could, genuine reciprocity, the ability to witness and validate the full complexity of grief, and the kind of authentic human connection that ultimately supports healing more effectively than any simulati on.[76 88] Sharing the experience of transitioning away from the digital tool with others who understand its significance transforms what might feel like a solitary struggle into a supported journey.[76]

The timeline for this transition varies considerably among individuals and should not be rushed to meet external expectations. What matters is not how quickly someone lets go, but whether the process moves them toward the internalized connection and meaning-making that characterize healthy grief.[76] Some people may complete this transition over weeks, others over months. The pace matters less than the direction, and that direction should always point toward greater engagement with present life while carrying the deceased forward in memory, values, and ongoing influence rather than through technological mediation.[87] Ella's story, which opened this chapter, illustrates a truth that many bereaved individuals discover only through experience. Letting go of a digital loved one is not a single moment of decision but a process that unfolds over time, requiring courage, support, and deep trust in the natural progression of grief. When Ella finally deactivated the AI version of Maya, she was not abandoning her daughter or betraying their relationship. She was honoring the transformation that healthy grief demands, the evolution from external connection maintained through technology to internalized presence carried forward in memory, values, and ongoing life.

This transformation represents what contemporary grief science tells us is essential for healthy bereavement. That is, the oscillation between engaging with loss and rebuilding life in the changed world, which is indicative of healthy grief adaptation. Digital loved ones can support this oscillation during certain phases of grief, providing connection when the absence feels unbearable while the bereaved person gradually develops internal resources for carrying the relationship forward. But there comes a point in many grief journeys when continued reliance on external digital connection begins to interfere with the restoration-oriented coping that allows life to move forward. Recognizing that point requires the kind of honest self-assessment this chapter has explored, paying attention to whether interactions still bring genuine comfort or have become hollow, whether the tool supports engagement with present life or serves as refuge from it, and whether the deceased has become sufficiently internalized that technological mediation is no longer necessary or helpful.

The process of letting go brings its own grief, a secondary loss that deserves acknowledgment even as we recognize its necessity. This reflects the genuine role these tools can play during acute grief and the authentic attachment that can form even to simulations when they provide comfort during devastating loss. The strategies this chapter has outlined, gradual reduction rather than abrupt cessation, development of alternative practices that serve similar emotional functions, creation of meaningful closure rituals, and maintenance of strong human support systems, all recognize that this transition requires deliberate care and compassion toward oneself.

What emerges on the other side of this transition is not absence but presence of a different kind. The internalized connection that develops as bereaved individuals step back from digital tools represents the continuing bond that grief research validates as both normal and healthy. The deceased remains part of who we are, influencing our choices, shaping our values, and living on in the ways we move through the world. This presence does not require technology to maintain it. It exists in the fabric of our identity, woven through years of relationship that death transforms but does not erase.

For readers currently using AI grief companions, this chapter offers both validation and guidance. If these tools are serving your healing during acute grief, providing connection while you develop internal resources for carrying your loved one forward, there is no need to rush toward letting go before you are ready. But if you recognize the signs this chapter has described, if interactions have begun to feel hollow or the tool has become a refuge from rather than support for engaging with life, it may be time to consider the transition this chapter explores. That transition is not abandonment but evolution, not forgetting but integrating, not an ending but a transformation of how you carry your loved one forward into the life you must continue to live. The wisdom to know when that time has come exists within you, supported by the frameworks this book has provided and the human connections that remain essential throughout every phase of grief.

Key points in Chapter Eleven

- Healthy grief eventually shifts from external forms of connection to internalised presence, where the deceased lives within memory, values, and identity.
- Signs that it is time to step back from AI include diminishing comfort, emotional dissonance, and a growing sense that the simulation no longer reflects the real relationship.
- Internalised connection strengthens as you begin to know instinctively how your loved one would respond, without needing technological mediation.
- Continued reliance on AI can interfere with restoration oriented coping by anchoring you in the past and preventing the natural evolution of grief.
- Letting go is a process that involves emotional courage, not a single moment of detachment, and it often brings its own form of secondary grief.
- Gradual reduction supports emotional stability and allows the internal bond to strengthen without abrupt disruption.
- Rituals of closure can honour the role the AI played while marking the transition toward a more integrated form of connection.
- This chapter guides readers through the shift from digital presence to inner continuity, which is essential for long term adaptation and meaning making.

Chapter Twelve

Designing Your Digital Legacy: Preparing for Your Own Afterlife

"To live in hearts we leave behind is not to die."
Thomas Campbell, Hallowed Ground

Rosa had always assumed that the most difficult decisions she would face as her mother grew older would involve the familiar terrain of ageing: medical care, finances, and the family home. These were the matters she had prepared herself for, the ones that appeared in conversations about wills and enduring powers of attorney. What she had not anticipated was that the most complex and emotionally fraught responsibility would emerge from something far less visible. When her mother suffered a minor stroke and could no longer manage her accounts, Rosa found herself confronted with the vast and disordered landscape of her mother's digital life. A worn notebook lay open on the kitchen table, filled with fragments of information that hinted at the scale of what lay ahead. There were usernames without passwords, passwords without context, and references to platforms Rosa had never heard of. The list was not a guide but a puzzle, and each entry opened onto a part of her mother's world that she had never been asked to navigate.

Once she gained access to her mother's primary email account, the magnitude of the task became unmistakable. The inbox held years of correspondence, photographs, medical documents, receipts, and intimate exchanges with friends and relatives. It was a dense archive of a life lived partly online, stretching across continents and decades. Rosa felt the weight of responsibility settle on her as she realised she had no guidance about what her mother would have wanted. Should these materials be preserved, shared, protected, or erased. Each possibility carried emotional and ethical implications, and none of them felt straightforward.

The questions we avoid until it is too late

Researchers who study digital mourning and online memorial culture have observed that most people significantly underestimate the size, complexity, and emotional significance of their digital footprint [60 61 62]. A single individual may leave behind thousands of digital artefacts, many of which hold meaning for loved ones and shape how relationships continue after death [63 64]. These traces can offer comfort, but they can also create distress or conflict when families are left to interpret them without direction. Rosa felt this tension immediately. Every folder she opened revealed another facet of her mother's life, and every decision about what to do with it felt like a choice that could not be undone.

Many of the digital systems themselves did not recognize that anything had changed. Her mother's accounts remained active, notifications continued to arrive, and automated reminders surfaced as if her mother were simply occupied rather than incapacitated. A birthday alert for a friend appeared on her mother's phone, followed by a prompt to revisit "memories from this day ten years ago." These algorithmic echoes of the past, generated without awareness of the present, are a defining feature of grief in the digital age [60 62]. They highlight the disjunction between physical absence and digital persistence, a gap that can intensify the emotional experience of loss.

This persistence also creates practical challenges. Without clear instructions, families often struggle to access accounts, manage data, or determine what should be preserved or deleted [61 62]. Rosa encountered automated verification loops that demanded her mother's confirmation, a requirement that was impossible to meet. The systems were designed to protect privacy, but they were not designed to accommodate incapacity or death. The result was a kind of administrative limbo in which Rosa was responsible for decisions she could not fully enact.

As she worked through the accounts, another concern began to surface. Unattended digital profiles, especially those containing personal or financial information, can become vulnerable to misuse. Recent legal and digital-estate scholarship has highlighted that unclear ownership, inactive oversight, and unprotected accounts can expose families to risks ranging from privacy breaches to financial harm [45 46 47 48]. More recent research has shown that identity theft targeting deceased individuals is a growing problem, driven by the persistence of personal data in systems that continue to treat the deceased as active users [89 90]. Consumer protection agencies have issued updated guidance warning families that unmonitored accounts can be exploited for credit fraud, benefits claims, or impersonation, particularly in the months immediately following a death [91]. Rosa did not need to understand the legal intricacies to sense the danger. The combination of open accounts, sensitive information, and the absence of clear authority created a vulnerability she had not previously considered.

What unsettled her most was the realisation that none of this had been discussed in advance. Her mother had been diligent about traditional estate planning, yet they had never spoken about what should happen to her digital materials. This silence is common. Many people still do not view their digital presence as something that requires preparation, even though it now shapes how they are remembered and how their relationships continue after death [60 62 63]. The result is that families are often left to make decisions in the dark, guided more by guesswork than by clarity.

Sitting at the kitchen table, surrounded by devices, notebooks, and open browser tabs, Rosa began to understand that digital legacy planning is not a peripheral concern. It is an extension of care, a way of protecting loved ones from emotional and practical burdens, and a means of ensuring that the digital traces of a life are handled with intention rather than left to chance. She also recognised that if she did not address her own digital footprint, her children would one day face the same uncertainty she was now confronting.

The question she had avoided for years finally came into focus. What will happen to my data when I am gone. What do I want my digital afterlife to look like. And how can I make those wishes clear while I am still here.

This chapter begins with Rosa's story not because it is unusual, but because it is becoming increasingly common. Our digital lives have grown so large, and so intertwined with our identities, that leaving them unplanned is no longer a neutral choice. It is a decision that shapes how we are remembered and how those we love must navigate the world we leave behind.

Understanding your digital footprint

Rosa had always known her mother used her phone for more than calls and messages, but she had never grasped the sheer scale of what that meant until she began sorting through it. What she found was not a collection of isolated accounts but an entire ecosystem of digital traces that had accumulated quietly over years. There were photos stored in multiple cloud services, documents saved automatically by apps she did not recognise, voice notes that captured fleeting thoughts, and message threads that stretched back through different devices and platforms. The more she uncovered, the clearer it became that her mother's digital presence was not a single entity but a network of overlapping identities, each shaped by the habits and technologies of a particular moment in her life.

Researchers have noted that this complexity is now the norm rather than the exception. Digital footprints have expanded dramatically in the past decade as everyday communication, memory-keeping, and administrative tasks have shifted online [60 61 62]. What once might have been contained in a few physical folders or photo albums is now dispersed across cloud servers, social media platforms, messaging apps, and automated backups. These traces are not simply records of activity. They are extensions of identity, shaped by the rhythms of daily life and the technologies that mediate it [82].

For families, this creates both opportunities and challenges. Digital materials can offer a rich and intimate portrait of a person's life, preserving moments that might otherwise have been lost. At the same time, the sheer volume of data can be overwhelming, especially when no one has been designated to manage it. Rosa found herself moving between admiration and exhaustion as she scrolled through her mother's photos and messages. There were images she had never seen, conversations she had not known about, and documents that revealed the quiet administrative labour her mother had carried alone. Each discovery deepened her understanding of her mother's life, yet each also raised questions about what should be kept, what should be shared, and what should remain private.

The emotional significance of digital traces is well documented. Studies of online mourning show that photos, messages, and posts often become central to how people maintain continuing bonds with the deceased [63 64]. These materials can provide comfort, connection, and a sense of ongoing presence, particularly in the early stages of grief. Yet they can also complicate the grieving process when they surface unexpectedly or when family members disagree about how they should be handled [60 62]. Rosa felt this complexity as she moved through her mother's accounts. Some images brought warmth and familiarity. Others felt too intimate to hold. Still others raised questions she could not answer.

The practical implications are equally significant. Digital platforms vary widely in how they handle inactive or deceased users, and many offer only limited options for memorialisation or account management [89 91]. Some services allow accounts to be converted into memorial profiles, while others require formal documentation before granting access or closure. A few provide no clear pathway at all. Rosa discovered that her mother's accounts were scattered across platforms with different policies, different security requirements, and different assumptions about who should have access. Without a clear digital directive, she was left to navigate these systems one by one, often encountering barriers that were designed to protect privacy but that now prevented her from fulfilling her responsibilities.

The legal landscape adds another layer of complexity. Recent analyses of digital-estate law highlight significant gaps in how jurisdictions define ownership, access rights, and responsibilities for digital remains [45 46 47 48]. In many regions, digital assets are not treated in the same way as physical property, and families may have limited authority to manage or close accounts without explicit consent. This lack of clarity can leave digital materials vulnerable, particularly when accounts remain active and unmonitored. The risk is not only emotional but also practical. Unattended accounts can be vulnerable to misuse, especially when personal data continues to circulate, a problem that has grown more visible in recent years as personal data continues to circulate long after a person becomes incapacitated or dies [95 96 97].

Rosa had not anticipated any of this. She had assumed that her mother's digital life would be manageable, perhaps even straightforward. Instead, she found herself navigating a landscape that was both deeply personal and structurally complex, shaped by technologies that had evolved faster than the social and legal frameworks surrounding them. The experience forced her to confront a reality that many people still overlook. A digital footprint is not simply a collection of files. It is a living system of memories, relationships, and data flows that continues to operate even when the person at its centre can no longer participate.

Understanding this is the first step in designing a digital legacy. It requires recognising the scope of one's digital presence, the emotional and cultural significance of digital traces, and the practical challenges that arise when these materials are left unmanaged. For Rosa, this understanding emerged slowly, through the intimate and often disorienting process of piecing together her mother's online world. It was a task she had not chosen, yet it revealed a truth that would shape the decisions she made for herself. A digital legacy does not create itself. It must be crafted with intention, clarity, and care.

Consent, boundaries and the ethics of being recreated

Rosa had always thought of consent as something that belonged to the living. It governed medical decisions, financial arrangements, and the ordinary negotiations of daily life. Yet as she moved deeper into her mother's digital world, she began to understand that consent extends far beyond the moment a person can speak for themselves. It shapes what happens to their data, their memories, and even their likeness after they are gone. The more she uncovered, the more she realised that her mother had never been asked, and had never said, what she wanted her digital presence to become.

This absence of guidance is increasingly common. As digital technologies have evolved, the question of whether a person wishes to be digitally resurrected, memorialised, or represented by an algorithm has become both ethically charged and deeply personal. Scholars examining the rise of grief technologies note that the boundaries between memory, simulation, and identity are becoming more porous, creating new dilemmas for families and for society [86 88 89]. Some people find comfort in digital tools that preserve a loved one's voice or messages, while others feel troubled by the idea that a person's data might be used to generate responses they never authorised. The ethical tension lies not in the technology itself, but in the uncertainty about what the deceased would have wanted.

Rosa found herself thinking about this as she scrolled through her mother's messages. There were voice notes her mother had recorded for herself, reminders written in her own cadence, and long conversations with friends that revealed her humour and her worries. These materials were intimate, and Rosa felt protective of them. She could not imagine feeding them into a system that might mimic her mother's voice or generate new messages in her name. Yet she also knew that others might feel differently. Some families actively seek out digital tools that allow them to maintain a sense of connection, especially in the early stages of grief [89 91]. The question is not whether such tools are inherently good or harmful, but whether they align with the values and wishes of the person they represent.

Ethicists have argued that digital resurrection technologies raise profound questions about autonomy, dignity, and the boundaries of personhood [93 94]. When a system generates new messages or conversations based on a person's data, it creates a representation that is neither entirely them nor entirely separate from them. This hybrid presence can blur the distinction between memory and simulation, especially for those who are grieving. Without explicit consent, the use of such technologies risks misrepresenting the deceased or creating emotional experiences they never intended to evoke. Rosa felt this intuitively. Her mother had been a private person, careful about what she shared and with whom. The idea of her voice being reconstructed by an algorithm felt like a violation of that privacy, even if the intention behind it was love.

The issue becomes even more complex when considering the potential for misuse. As digital-estate scholars have noted, the same data that can be used to create comforting memorials can also be exploited in ways that undermine a person's dignity or expose their family to harm [45 46 47 48]. Identity theft targeting deceased individuals has become a growing concern, fuelled by the persistence of personal data in systems that continue to treat the deceased as active users [95 97]. Consumer protection agencies now warn families to secure or close accounts promptly, not only to protect financial information but also to prevent impersonation or unauthorised digital activity [96]. In this context, consent is not only an ethical matter but a practical safeguard.

Rosa realised that consent is not something that can be assumed or retroactively inferred. It must be articulated clearly, documented intentionally, and communicated to the people who will one day be responsible for carrying it out. This includes decisions about whether one wishes to be digitally recreated, whether one's voice or messages may be used in memorial technologies, and how one's data should be handled after death. These decisions are deeply personal, shaped by cultural beliefs, spiritual values, and individual comfort with technology. What matters is not that everyone makes the same choice, but that each person has the opportunity to make their own.

As Rosa reflected on her mother's silence, she began to consider her own wishes. She realised that she did not want her children to face the same uncertainty she was now navigating. She wanted them to know where she stood on digital resurrection, what she considered private, and how she wanted her digital presence to be managed. She wanted to spare them the burden of guessing. The more she thought about it, the clearer it became that consent is not only about autonomy. It is an act of care, a way of easing the emotional and practical load for those who will one day be left behind.

In the emerging landscape of digital afterlife technologies, consent is the foundation upon which ethical practice must rest. It is the difference between a digital legacy that honours a person's values and one that inadvertently distorts them. For Rosa, understanding this was the turning point. It marked the moment she shifted from reacting to her mother's digital footprint to actively shaping her own.

Preparing an ethical, emotionally safe digital legacy

As Rosa continued sorting through her mother's accounts, she began to realise that the question was no longer simply what existed, but what should remain. The digital traces she encountered were not neutral artefacts. They carried emotional weight, cultural meaning, and the potential to shape how her mother would be remembered. Some messages revealed her mother's private fears during the early days of her illness. Others captured moments of joy that Rosa had forgotten. There were photos that felt like gifts and others that felt like intrusions. The more she saw, the more she understood that a digital legacy is not just a collection of files. It is a landscape of memories that can either support or complicate the grieving process.

Recent research on digital grief underscores this complexity. Studies examining how people engage with digital remains show that photos, messages, and online profiles often become central to how relationships continue after death [60 62 82]. These materials can offer comfort, especially when they reflect the person's values and personality in ways that feel authentic. Yet they can also create distress when they surface unexpectedly, contain unresolved emotional content, or reveal aspects of the person's life that family members were not prepared to encounter [61 63]. Rosa found herself moving between these poles. Some discoveries brought her closer to her mother. Others left her shaken, unsure whether she was trespassing on something her mother had never intended to share.

This tension is not unique to Rosa. It reflects a broader shift in how grief unfolds in a digital age. Scholars have noted that digital traces can act as both anchors and disruptions, depending on how they are curated and contextualised [60 62 64]. When handled with care, they can help families maintain a sense of connection, honour the person's memory, and navigate the early stages of loss. When left unmanaged, they can overwhelm loved ones with volume, ambiguity, or emotional intensity. The difference often lies in whether the person took steps to shape their digital legacy before they died.

Preparing an ethical and emotionally safe digital legacy begins with intentionality. It requires thinking not only about what should be preserved, but why. Some people choose to leave behind a curated selection of photos, letters, or voice notes that reflect the parts of their life they want others to remember. Others prefer to limit what remains, believing that privacy in death is as important as privacy in life. There is no universal right answer. What matters is that the choices align with the person's values and the needs of the people who will inherit their digital presence.

Rosa realised that her mother had never been given the opportunity to make these choices. Her digital materials had accumulated organically, shaped by the technologies she used and the habits she developed over time. Without guidance, Rosa was left to interpret what should be kept and what should be allowed to fade. She found herself wishing her mother had left even a few notes about what mattered to her, what she considered private, and what she hoped her family would remember. That absence became a quiet lesson. A digital legacy is not something that emerges on its own. It must be crafted deliberately, with an understanding of how it will be experienced by others.

The ethical dimension of this work extends beyond emotional considerations. Digital-estate specialists emphasise that unmanaged accounts can expose families to privacy breaches, legal complications, and even identity theft [45] [46] [47] [48] [95] [96] [97]. Photos stored in unsecured cloud folders, documents containing personal information, and accounts left active without oversight can all become points of vulnerability. Preparing a digital legacy therefore involves not only curating what should remain, but securing or removing what should not. This includes deleting outdated accounts, organising important documents, and ensuring that sensitive information is protected.

For Rosa, this realisation marked a turning point. She began to think not only about her mother's legacy, but about her own. She imagined her children sitting where she sat now, trying to make sense of her digital life without guidance. The thought unsettled her. She wanted to spare them the burden, the emotional labour, and the risk of encountering things she would never have wanted them to see. She wanted to leave behind something that felt intentional, coherent, and kind.

Preparing an ethical digital legacy is ultimately an act of care. It acknowledges that our digital lives have become intertwined with our identities, our relationships, and the ways we are remembered. It recognises that the traces we leave behind can either support or burden the people we love. And it affirms that we have the ability, and the responsibility, to shape that legacy while we are still here.

For Rosa, this understanding did not erase the difficulty of sorting through her mother's accounts. But it gave her a sense of purpose. Each decision she made became part of a larger commitment to honour her mother's values and to ensure that her own digital presence would one day be easier for her children to navigate. In that sense, preparing a digital legacy is not only about death. It is about the relationships that continue, the memories that endure, and the care we extend across time.

Practical steps for digital legacy planning

By the time Rosa had worked through the first wave of her mother's accounts, she understood that intention alone was not enough. Care, clarity, and ethical awareness mattered, but without practical structures to support them, even the most thoughtful wishes could become difficult to carry out. Digital legacy planning requires more than a general sense of what one wants. It demands concrete steps that translate values into actions, and preferences into instructions that others can follow. As Rosa began to consider her own digital footprint, she realised that the work ahead was not only emotional but administrative, and that the two were more closely intertwined than she had ever imagined.

The first step in designing a digital legacy is taking stock of what exists. Most people underestimate the number of accounts they hold and the volume of data stored across platforms [60 61 62]. Email services, social media profiles, cloud storage systems, banking apps, subscription platforms, and digital photo libraries all accumulate quietly over time. Rosa recognised that she had accounts she had not used in years, documents saved automatically by apps she barely remembered, and photos scattered across multiple devices. Creating an inventory became the foundation of her planning. It allowed her to see the scope of her digital presence and to identify which accounts mattered, which could be closed, and which required careful handling.

Once the inventory is established, the next step is clarifying access. Digital-estate specialists emphasise that without clear instructions, families often struggle to manage or close accounts, even when they have legal authority to do so [45 46 47 48]. Password managers have become an increasingly important tool in this process, offering a secure way to store login information and designate trusted contacts. Some platforms now allow users to nominate a legacy contact who can manage or memorialise an account after death [89 91]. Rosa found this feature reassuring. It offered a way to ensure that her children would not face the same barriers she had encountered, and it allowed her to specify what level of access she wanted them to have.

Documenting one's wishes is equally essential. A digital will or data directive provides formal guidance about how digital materials should be handled, including which accounts should be preserved, which should be deleted, and how sensitive information should be protected [46 47]. These documents can also specify whether a person consents to the use of their data in memorial technologies, AI-driven simulations, or digital-afterlife services [93 94]. Rosa realised that without such documentation, her children would be left to interpret her intentions, just as she had been left to interpret her mother's. Writing down her preferences became an act of clarity, a way of ensuring that her values would be honoured even when she could no longer articulate them.

Security is another critical component of digital legacy planning. Unattended accounts can become vulnerable to misuse, particularly in the months following a death when personal information may still be circulating through automated systems [95 97]. Consumer protection agencies now advise families to close or secure accounts promptly, monitor for unusual activity, and ensure that sensitive documents are stored in protected locations [96]. Rosa had seen first-hand how easily an account could be accessed by someone with malicious intent. An unfamiliar login attempt on her mother's profile had been a turning point, a reminder that digital vulnerability does not end with death. Incorporating security measures into her own planning felt not only prudent but necessary.

Finally, digital legacy planning requires communication. Even the most carefully crafted documents can create confusion if loved ones do not know they exist or do not understand their purpose. Rosa began to speak with her children about her digital life, explaining where her accounts were, how she used them, and what she wanted done with them in the future. These conversations were not always easy, but they brought a sense of relief. They transformed her digital legacy from a private burden into a shared understanding, one that her children could carry with confidence rather than uncertainty.

Practical steps do not diminish the emotional significance of digital legacy planning. They support it. They provide the structure that allows values to be honoured, memories to be preserved, and vulnerabilities to be addressed. For Rosa, taking these steps became part of a broader commitment to care. It was a way of ensuring that her digital presence would not become a source of difficulty or risk, but a reflection of the life she had lived and the relationships she cherished.

Digital legacy planning is not a task to be completed in a single sitting. It is an ongoing process, shaped by new technologies, changing circumstances, and evolving relationships. Yet the steps are clear. Take stock of what exists. Clarify access. Document wishes. Secure accounts. Communicate with those who will one day be responsible. These actions form the foundation of a digital legacy that is intentional, ethical, and emotionally grounded. They allow us to shape the traces we leave behind and to offer our loved ones the clarity and care they deserve.

When to seek legal advice

As Rosa moved further into her mother's digital accounts, she began to realise that the emotional and practical challenges she faced were only part of a larger landscape. Beneath the surface of every login attempt and every unanswered security question lay a set of legal questions she had never considered. Who owned the photos stored in her mother's cloud accounts. Who had the right to close her social media profiles. What counted as personal property, and what belonged to the platform. These were not abstract concerns. They shaped what Rosa could do, what she was allowed to do, and what she might inadvertently risk by acting without guidance.

In recent years, legal scholars and digital-estate specialists have emphasised that the law has struggled to keep pace with the rapid expansion of digital life [45 46 47 48]. Traditional estate frameworks were built around physical assets, not cloud-based archives or algorithmically generated content. As a result, the rules governing digital remains vary widely across jurisdictions, and the boundaries between personal property, intellectual property, and platform-controlled data are often unclear. Rosa discovered this first hand when she attempted to close one of her mother's accounts and was told she needed documentation that did not exist, while another platform allowed her to proceed with little more than a death certificate. The inconsistency was disorienting, and it underscored how essential legal clarity had become.

The need for legal advice becomes even more pressing when considering the risks associated with unmanaged digital estates. Identity theft targeting deceased individuals has become a growing concern, driven by the persistence of personal data in systems that continue to treat the deceased as active users [95 97]. Consumer protection agencies now warn families that unmonitored accounts can be exploited for credit fraud, benefits claims, or impersonation, particularly in the months immediately following a death [96]. For Rosa, the unfamiliar login attempt on her mother's account was no longer just alarming. It was a sign that legal and security considerations were intertwined, and that acting without proper guidance could expose her family to risks she had not anticipated.

Legal advice can help families navigate these complexities with confidence. A lawyer familiar with digital-estate planning can clarify which assets are covered by existing wills, which require separate directives, and how to ensure that a person's wishes are legally enforceable. They can explain the differences between digital assets, digital remains, and intellectual property, and help families understand how platform policies interact with local laws. They can also assist in drafting digital wills or data directives that specify how accounts should be managed, who should have access, and what should be preserved or deleted. These documents provide clarity not only for families but for the platforms that must interpret and act on them.

For individuals preparing their own digital legacy, legal advice offers a way to ensure that their intentions are honoured. It allows them to document their preferences in a way that carries legal weight, reducing the burden on loved ones and minimising the risk of disputes or misunderstandings. It also provides an opportunity to address issues that might otherwise be overlooked, such as the treatment of digital assets with financial value, the management of professional accounts, or the handling of data stored in multiple jurisdictions.

Rosa found that speaking with a lawyer transformed her understanding of what digital legacy planning required. It shifted the work from a series of reactive decisions to a coherent strategy grounded in clarity and protection. It also gave her the confidence to begin shaping her own digital directive, knowing that her choices would be supported by a legal framework rather than left to interpretation.

Seeking legal advice is not a sign that digital legacy planning is too complex to manage alone. It is a recognition that the digital world has introduced new forms of property, new forms of vulnerability, and new forms of remembrance that deserve careful consideration. It ensures that the decisions we make about our digital lives are not only thoughtful but enforceable, and that the people we leave behind are supported rather than burdened.

For Rosa, this understanding became part of the larger lesson her mother's digital life had taught her. Care is not only emotional. It is structural, legal and protective. And it is something we owe to the people who will one day navigate the traces we leave behind.

A final note on intention

By the time Rosa finished working through her mother's accounts, she understood that the task had been about far more than passwords or platforms. It had been an intimate encounter with the traces of a life lived partly online, a reminder that our digital presence carries emotional weight long after we stop tending to it. Some of what she found brought comfort. Some of it raised questions she could not answer. All of it revealed how deeply our digital habits shape the way we are remembered.

What stayed with her most was the realisation that clarity is a gift. Her mother had not been given the chance to articulate what mattered, what was private, or what she hoped her family would preserve. That silence made every decision heavier. Rosa did not want her children to inherit the same uncertainty. She wanted them to know her intentions, not guess at them.

Digital legacy planning is often framed as a technical exercise, but at its heart it is an act of care. It allows us to shape the story that remains, to protect the people we love from unnecessary burdens, and to ensure that our digital presence reflects our values rather than the accidents of what we leave behind. It does not require perfection. It requires intention.

Rosa's experience is becoming increasingly common, and it offers a simple truth: our digital lives will outlast us in ways we may not expect. The choices we make now can ease the path for those who follow. With that in mind, the next section offers a practical template to help you begin shaping your own digital legacy with clarity and confidence.

Key points in Chapter Twelve

- Most people underestimate the size, complexity, and emotional significance of their digital footprint, which can leave families overwhelmed and unprepared.
- Unmanaged accounts create emotional, practical, and security risks, including identity theft, privacy breaches, and confusion about what should be preserved or deleted.
- Digital legacy planning requires intentional curation rather than passive accumulation, because digital traces shape how relationships continue after death.
- Consent about digital resurrection, data use, and posthumous representation must be explicit, documented, and communicated to loved ones.
- Ethical legacy design involves protecting dignity, privacy, and autonomy while considering the emotional needs of those who will inherit your digital presence.
- Practical steps include creating an inventory of accounts, clarifying access, documenting wishes, securing sensitive information, and closing unused platforms.
- Communication with loved ones ensures that your intentions are understood and prevents the uncertainty that often burdens families during grief.
- This chapter reframes digital legacy planning as an act of care that supports both memory and emotional wellbeing for future generations.

Chapter Thirteen

The Future of Grief and Technology: Navigating Change With Wisdom

"Nothing endures but change."

Heraclitus

Ilsa stood in the virtual reality memorial space, surrounded by softly rendered versions of the places she and her late husband, Jordan, had loved. The environment wasn't photorealistic, but it was recognisable; a curated digital memorial room built from photos, videos, and audio clips she had provided. Two years had passed since Jordan's death, and in that time Ilsa had navigated her grief through therapy, a bereavement group, and careful self-reflection. She had briefly used an AI chatbot built from Jordan's old messages, a tool that had helped her revisit certain memories before she recognised it was time to let it go. She had worked through the BONDS Framework, established healthy boundaries, and gradually internalised her connection with Jordan in ways that supported her ongoing life. She thought she understood the landscape of grief technology reasonably well.

Yet here she stood, participating in a research study that introduced her to tools she had not encountered before. The VR memorial space was one example; a digital environment designed for remembrance rather than simulation. The research team also showed her prototypes of grief-support apps that used AI to offer personalised coping suggestions, and early versions of holographic memorial displays used in some funeral services. They mentioned speculative technologies still years away, such as advanced holograms or brain-computer interfaces that might one day simulate emotional states, but they were clear that these remained future possibilities rather than present-day tools.

The experience raised questions that extended far beyond this particular virtual park where Jordan had once proposed. Technology would continue to evolve, bringing innovations that none of them could yet fully imagine. Some would be subtle refinements of existing tools, while others might fundamentally reshape how humans engage with loss and memory. The pace of change seemed relentless, and Ilsa wondered how anyone could possibly keep up, let alone make wise decisions about which tools to embrace and which to avoid.

This chapter explores the evolving landscape of grief support technology while grounding readers in the enduring principles that should guide their engagement with emerging tools. The technologies may change, but the fundamental nature of grief remains constant, as do the core principles of healthy bereavement established throughout this book. Understanding this distinction between what changes and what endures is essential for navigating an uncertain technological future with wisdom and discernment.

The chapter also examines anticipated developments in AI and digital bereavement technologies, from increasingly sophisticated simulations to virtual reality memorialisation and predictive grief support systems. Yet rather than simply cataloguing innovations, it emphasises how the frameworks and principles explored in previous chapters, particularly the BONDS Framework and clinical grief models, provide a stable foundation for evaluating any new tool that emerges. The questions that matter most are not about what technology can do, but about what serves authentic healing, honours the complexity of loss, and supports the deeply human work of integrating grief into ongoing life.

As you read this chapter, you will discover that the wisdom required to navigate future grief technologies is not primarily technological but human. It is grounded in self-awareness, clinical understanding of grief processes, ethical principles, and the courage to make choices aligned with your values. The future will bring new tools, but you have agency in deciding what to use, when to engage, and how to integrate technologies in ways that support your healing rather than complicate it. This chapter prepares you to approach emerging innovations with both curiosity and critical evaluation, ensuring that regardless of how technology evolves, you remain grounded in the timeless work of learning to live with loss while still engaging fully with life.

Emerging technologies in grief support: What's coming and what it means

The technologies emerging in grief support extend far beyond the chatbots and text-based AI companions that have dominated in recent years. Research teams are developing increasingly sophisticated tools that engage multiple senses and create immersive experiences of connection. Virtual reality memorial spaces, like the one Ilsa explored, represent just one category of innovation.[92] Voice synthesis technology has advanced to the point where it can recreate a deceased person's vocal patterns from relatively limited audio samples, allowing bereaved individuals to hear their loved one's voice speaking new words they never actually said.[93] Holographic displays, still in the early stages of development but rapidly improving, promise three-dimensional visual representations that could appear in physical spaces rather than requiring headsets or screens.

These developments raise questions that go beyond the ethical considerations explored in earlier chapters. When technology can recreate not just text-based conversation but voice, visual presence, and even simulated physical environments, the psychological impact intensifies correspondingly.[92 93] The human brain processes visual and auditory information differently than text, engaging emotional centres more directly and creating stronger illusions of presence. Research in human-computer interaction demonstrates that multisensory experiences generate more powerful emotional responses and stronger attachment, which means these emerging tools carry both greater potential for comfort and greater risk of dependency or complicated grief.[92 93]

Artificial intelligence systems are also becoming more sophisticated in their ability to provide personalised grief support beyond simply mimicking a deceased person's communication style.[92 93] Machine learning algorithms can now analyse patterns in how individuals express and process grief, offering tailored coping suggestions, identifying potential warning signs of complicated bereavement, and adapting their responses based on the user's emotional state and grief trajectory.[92] Some experimental systems integrate with wearable devices to monitor physiological markers of stress or emotional dysregulation, potentially alerting users or their support networks when intervention might be needed. These predictive capabilities promise more responsive support but also raise profound questions about privacy, autonomy, and the appropriate role of algorithmic systems in such deeply personal experiences.[93]

The grief technology landscape is also expanding to include tools that blend digital innovation with traditional memorial practices.[94] Some funeral homes now offer digital memorial services that combine physical ceremonies with livestreamed participation, archived recordings, and interactive tribute spaces where attendees can share memories and condolences long after the service concludes.[94] Memorial jewellery has evolved to include pieces that can store and play audio recordings, display scrolling text messages, or even incorporate biometric data like fingerprints or heartbeat patterns.[94] These hybrid approaches acknowledge that grief exists simultaneously in physical and digital realms, and that meaningful memorialisation might draw on both.[94]

What matters most about these emerging technologies is not their technical sophistication but how they intersect with the core processes of healthy grief. The Dual Process Model of Grief, Continuing Bonds Theory, and other clinical frameworks explored throughout this book remain relevant regardless of how advanced the technology becomes.[93] The questions that should guide evaluation of any new tool are timeless. Does it support oscillation between loss-oriented and restoration-oriented coping, or does it anchor someone too firmly in the past? Does it facilitate the transformation from external to internalised connection, or does it prevent that essential transition? Does it complement human support systems and professional guidance, or does it become a substitute for them?[92 95] Does it honour the deceased person's dignity and autonomy, or does it risk distorting their memory in service of the bereaved person's needs? [93] These questions provide a stable foundation for navigating technological change, ensuring that innovation serves healing rather than complicating it.[92 93]

Enduring principles for evaluating new tools: Applying wisdom to innovation

The rapid evolution of grief technology can feel overwhelming, as though each new innovation requires learning an entirely new framework for evaluation. Yet the wisdom required to assess these tools is not technological but deeply human, rooted in principles that remain constant regardless of how sophisticated the simulations become.[96] These enduring principles provide a stable foundation for navigating change, ensuring that you maintain agency and discernment even as the technological landscape shifts beneath your feet.

The first principle centres on authenticity and the nature of relationship. Healthy human connections are characterised by reciprocity, unpredictability, and genuine mutual influence.[96 16] When evaluating any grief technology, ask whether it supports authentic connection or creates an illusion that ultimately isolates you from real relationships. This question applies equally to today's text-based chatbots and tomorrow's holographic projections. The Dual Process Model of

Grief, explored in earlier chapters, emphasises that grief requires oscillation between engaging with loss and rebuilding life in the present. Technologies that anchor you too firmly in the past, regardless of how emotionally compelling they feel, work against this fundamental process.[96 16] The sophistication of the simulation matters far less than whether it supports your movement through grief or prevents it.

The second principle concerns consent and dignity, both for the deceased and for yourself. Any technology that recreates a person's likeness, voice, or communication patterns raises questions about whether that person would have agreed to such use of their digital traces.[96 16] This ethical consideration does not disappear simply because the technology becomes more advanced or widely accepted. In fact, as capabilities expand to include voice synthesis, visual representation, and even predictive responses based on personality modelling, the stakes of consent become higher. You must ask not only whether you have the legal right to use someone's data, but whether doing so honours their autonomy and the complexity of who they were. Equally important is your own dignity and wellbeing. Technologies that exploit vulnerability or encourage dependency, regardless of how comforting they initially feel, ultimately undermine your capacity for healthy grief adaptation.[16]

The third principle emphasises integration within human support systems rather than technological isolation. The BONDS Framework introduced in Chapter 10 includes Social Embedding as a core element precisely because grief healing happens within communities of care, not in solitary interaction with algorithms. This principle applies to every emerging tool you encounter. Before engaging with any new technology, ask how it will fit within your existing support network. Will it complement your therapy sessions, your grief group participation, your connections with friends and family? Or will it become a substitute for these vital human relationships? Technologies that promise to meet all your emotional needs independently should be approached with particular caution, as they risk creating the kind of isolation that complicates rather than supports bereavemen t.[16]

The fourth principle involves recognising the limits of simulation and the importance of accepting death's finality.[96] Grief ultimately requires integrating loss into your ongoing life, transforming external connection into internalised memory and meaning.[96 16] Technologies that implicitly suggest they eliminate the pain of loss or maintain unchanged relationships with the deceased work against this critical process. As you evaluate new tools, ask whether they support the difficult but necessary work of acceptance, or whether they offer escape from that work.[96] The most sophisticated simulation remains wholly different from the person you lost, and technologies that blur this distinction risk preventing the transformation of grief that allows you to move forward while still honouring your loved one's memory.[16 97]

These principles provide a framework for evaluating not just current technologies but innovations that have not yet emerged. They ground your decision-making in timeless wisdom about grief, relationship, dignity, and healing, ensuring that regardless of how technology evolves, you remain anchored in what truly supports your wellbeing.[96]

Building your personal framework for the future: Agency, discernment and authentic healing

The wisdom required to navigate grief technology, now and in the future, is not about mastering algorithms or predicting innovations. It is about understanding yourself with honesty and compassion, knowing what you need at different points in your grief journey, and maintaining the courage to make decisions aligned with your values rather than succumbing to technological seduction or cultural pressure. Building your personal framework means developing the capacity to evaluate any tool, current or future, through the lens of what truly serves your healing.

This framework begins with agency, the recognition that you retain control over your grief process regardless of what technologies become available.[15] [16] Agency means deciding whether to engage with digital tools at all, setting boundaries around how and when you use them, and maintaining the right to step back or disengage entirely when something no longer serves you.[15] It means resisting the subtle pressure that can emerge when grief technologies become normalised or commercialised, when companies market products that promise to ease your pain or when well-meaning friends suggest tools that worked for them.[19] [16] Your grief is yours alone, and no external authority, technological or otherwise, can determine the right path for your healing. The question is never what you should do according to some universal standard, but what supports your unique process of integrating loss into your ongoing life.

Discernment builds on agency by providing the critical evaluation skills necessary to distinguish between tools that support healing and those that complicate it.[15] [16] This requires understanding the difference between comfort and avoidance, between maintaining continuing bonds and preventing necessary transformation, between using technology as one element within a broader support system and allowing it to become a substitute for human connection. Discernment means asking difficult questions before, during, and after engaging with any grief technology. Does this tool support my oscillation between loss-oriented and restoration-oriented coping, or does it anchor me too firmly in the past? Does it facilitate the transformation from external to internalised connection, or does it prevent that essential transition?[15] Does it honour the deceased person's dignity and autonomy, or does it risk distorting their memory?[15] Does it complement my therapy, my grief group, my relationships with living people, or does it isolate me further?

These questions apply equally to the chatbot you might use today and the holographic projection you might encounter tomorrow. The technology changes, but the principles remain constant because they are grounded in the enduring nature of grief itself. Healthy bereavement requires accepting death's finality, reconstructing meaning in a world forever altered by loss, and gradually internalising your connection with the deceased so that they live on in your values, choices, and ongoing life rather than through external dependencies.[16] Any technology that works against these processes, regardless of how emotionally compelling or technologically sophisticated it may be, ultimately hinders rather than supports your healing.[15]

Authentic healing, the third pillar of your personal framework, means prioritising the internal work of grief over the external comfort that technology can provide.[16] It means recognising that the pain of loss, while excruciating, serves a purpose in helping you integrate what has happened and adapt to life without the person you loved. Technologies that promise to eliminate this pain or maintain unchanged relationships with the deceased may offer temporary relief, but they risk preventing the transformation that allows you to move forward while still honouring your loved one's memory.[16] Authentic healing happens in the messy, difficult, deeply human work of sitting with grief, processing it within communities of care, and gradually discovering how to carry your loss without being consumed by it.[19] Technology can support this work, but it can never replace it.

As Ilsa removed the VR headset and stepped back into the research facility's waiting room, she carried with her a clarity that had taken two years of grief work to develop. The virtual memorial space had been beautiful, technically impressive, and emotionally evocative. Yet she recognised that she no longer needed it. The memories it recreated already lived within her, woven into the fabric of who she had become since Jordan's death. This recognition represented not a rejection of technology but an understanding of where she was in her grief journey and what genuinely served her healing at this particular moment.

The future will bring technologies none of us can fully anticipate. Virtual reality environments will become more immersive, artificial intelligence more sophisticated in mimicking human communication, and new innovations will emerge that blur the boundaries between memory and simulation in ways we cannot yet imagine. Companies will market these tools with promises of comfort and connection, and some bereaved individuals will find genuine value in them during specific phases of their grief. Others will discover, as Ilsa did, that the most meaningful connection exists not in technological recreations but in the internalised bonds that shape how we live, choose, and move through the world after loss.

What matters most is not predicting which technologies will emerge or mastering their technical specifications, but maintaining the wisdom to evaluate any tool through the lens of what supports authentic healing. The BONDS Framework, the clinical grief models explored throughout this book, and the principles of healthy bereavement provide a stable foundation regardless of how rapidly technology evolves. These frameworks are not about restricting your choices but about empowering you to make decisions grounded in self-awareness, clinical understanding, and alignment with your values rather than reacting to technological seduction or cultural pressure.

The questions that should guide your engagement with grief technology, now and in the future, remain constant. Does this tool support your oscillation between engaging with loss and rebuilding life in the present? Does it facilitate the transformation from external connection to internalised memory and meaning? Does it complement your human support systems and professional guidance, or does it risk becoming a substitute for them? Does it honour both your dignity and the dignity of the person you have lost? These questions apply equally to the chatbot you might use today and the holographic projection you might encounter tomorrow, because they are grounded in the fundamental nature of grief itself rather than the specifics of any particular technology.

You have agency in this rapidly changing landscape. You can choose what to use, when to engage, and how to integrate tools in ways that support your healing rather than complicate it. You can set boundaries, seek professional guidance, maintain human connections, and step back from technologies that no longer serve you. You can honour your loved one's memory through the choices you make, the values you carry forward, and the life you continue to build even in their absence. No algorithm, regardless of how sophisticated it becomes, can replicate the depth of human connection or replace the essential work of learning to live with loss.

The future of grief and technology is uncertain, but the wisdom required to navigate it is timeless. It lives not in technical expertise but in self-knowledge, compassion, discernment, and the courage to make choices aligned with what genuinely supports your healing. As you move forward, trust that wisdom. Trust your capacity to evaluate new tools critically. Trust that the most important work of grief happens not in digital spaces but in the deeply human process of accepting loss, reconstructing meaning, and discovering how to carry what you have lost into the life that continues.

Key points in Chapter Thirteen

- Emerging technologies such as virtual reality memorials, holographic representations, and predictive grief support systems will expand the possibilities for digital remembrance.
- Multisensory simulations may intensify emotional impact, which increases both their potential benefits and their psychological risks.
- Ethical questions about consent, dignity, and representation will grow more complex as technology becomes more immersive and more capable of mimicking human presence.
- Clinical grief principles remain stable even as technology evolves, which means the core work of grief does not change.
- The BONDS Framework provides a timeless guide for evaluating new tools, ensuring that decisions remain grounded in psychological safety and ethical clarity.
- Agency allows individuals to choose how and when to engage with technology rather than being swept along by cultural trends or commercial pressure.
- Discernment helps distinguish between tools that support healing and those that offer comfort at the cost of long term adaptation.
- Authentic healing remains rooted in human connection, internal meaning making, and the gradual integration of loss into ongoing life, regardless of technological innovation.

Conclusion

If you have reached this final page, you have travelled through territory that would have been unimaginable to previous generations of grieving people. You have explored technologies that can simulate voices, recreate conversational patterns, and offer the illusion of continued connection with those who have died. You have examined the psychological mechanisms that make these tools feel powerful, the ethical complexities they raise, and the practical frameworks for using them safely. Most importantly, you have been asked to think deeply about your own grief, your own needs, and your own capacity to navigate loss in an age where technology offers both unprecedented comfort and unprecedented risk.

The central question this book has explored is not whether AI grief companions are good or bad in some universal sense. Technology itself is neutral. The question that matters is whether these tools serve your healing at this particular moment in your grief journey, and whether you can engage with them in ways that support rather than hinder the difficult, essential work of integrating loss into your ongoing life.

What grief science tells us, consistently and clearly, is that healthy bereavement involves both confronting the reality of loss and rebuilding a life that moves forward. It requires oscillation between engaging with grief and stepping back into restoration. It demands the gradual transformation of external connection into internalized bonds that shape who you are and how you live. It needs human support, professional guidance when necessary, and the courage to sit with pain rather than constantly seeking escape from it. These principles do not change regardless of what technologies emerge. They are supported by decades of clinical research and in the timeless human experience of learning to live with loss.

AI grief companions can support this process when used with clear boundaries, honest self-assessment, and integration within broader support systems. They can offer comfort during acute grief, help preserve memories, and provide a bridge through the most devastating early months of bereavement. But they can also become obstacles to healing when they enable avoidance, create dependency, or prevent the acceptance that loss requires. The difference lies not in the technology itself, but in how, when, and why you use it.

The BONDS Framework offers a structure for making these decisions with wisdom rather than desperation. It asks you to establish boundaries that protect your emotional wellbeing, to consider consent and dignity in how you represent the deceased, to prioritize neuropsychological safety by recognizing warning signs of unhealthy use, to ensure justice in how memory is preserved, and to embed any digital tool within living human relationships rather than using it in isolation. This framework does not tell you what to do, but it gives you the questions to ask and the principles to guide your choices.

As technology continues to evolve, you will encounter tools and possibilities that do not yet exist. Virtual reality memorials may become more immersive. AI simulations may become more sophisticated. New forms of digital connection may emerge that we cannot yet imagine. But the wisdom you need to evaluate these tools is already within your reach. It lies in understanding your own grief pattern, in recognizing what supports healthy adaptation, in maintaining human connection, and in trusting yourself to make choices aligned with your values and your healing.

Grief is not a problem technology can solve. It is a profound human experience that requires time, support, courage, and the willingness to be transformed by loss. Digital tools may accompany you on that journey, but they cannot replace the deeply human work of learning to carry love and loss together as you move forward into life. You have the knowledge, the framework, and the agency to navigate this landscape with wisdom. Trust yourself, seek support when you need it, and remember that healing does not mean forgetting. It means learning to live fully even as you carry the memory of those you have lost.

About the author

Sera Vale is a writer and behavioural thinker whose work examines how human beings evolve, adapt, and make meaning in a world defined by rapid change. Trained in anthropology and shaped by a career spent advising leaders and organisations, she brings a uniquely multidimensional perspective to human behaviour: One that spans deep time, cultural history, and the everyday realities of modern life.

Her approach is grounded in the belief that to understand why people act as they do today, we must look not only at contemporary pressures but also at the long arc of human development. By drawing on insights from evolutionary psychology, social science, and organisational research, she illuminates the enduring motives and patterns that continue to influence how we think, relate, and lead.

Sera's writing is known for its clarity, depth, and practical relevance. She translates complex ideas into accessible frameworks that help readers navigate uncertainty, strengthen their decision-making, and understand themselves and others with greater nuance. Whether exploring workplace dynamics, leadership challenges, or the psychological impact of emerging technologies, her work invites readers to see human behaviour with fresh perspective and informed curiosity.

References

1. Haring, C.. (2024, July 2). *Finding Support in Grief Through Technological Advancements*. Death with Dignity. https://deathwithdignity.org/news/2024/07/tech-advancements-to-end-of-life/

2. Cooper, S.. (2023, December). *The benefits and challenges of grieving online*. Counseling Today. https://www.counseling.org/publications/counseling-today-magazine/article-archive/article/legacy/the-benefits-and-challenges-of-grieving-online

3. Fusco, R., Ciliberti, R., Licata, M., & Picozzi, M.. (n.d.). *Ritual and mourning in the digital era: Between virtual technology and ethical controversies*. Acta Biomedica. https://mattioli1885journals.com/index.php/actabiomedica/article/download/15994/12008/121871

4. Lawrence, C.. (2021, February 02). *How has the digital age affected the way we grieve?*. SANE. https://www.sane.org.uk/how-we-help/sane-community/your-blogs/how-has-the-digital-age-affected-the-way-we-grieve

5. Bates, D.. (2024, August 18). *Navigating Grief in the Digital Age*. Psychology Today. https://www.psychologytoday.com/us/blog/mental-health-nerd/202408/navigating-grief-in-the-digital-age

6. Townley Wheeler Funeral Home. (2025, February 07). *Grief in the Digital Age*. Townley Wheeler Funeral Home. https://www.townleywheelerfh.com/accoutrements/blog-theres-morgue-to-it/grief-in-the-digital-age

7. Zainutdinova, A.. (2025, September 10). *Grief in the digital age: the AI dilemma*. Meer. https://www.meer.com/en/91771-grief-in-the-digital-age-the-ai-dilemma

8. Roamers Therapy. (n.d.). *Understanding Grief: A Journey of Adaptation*. Roamers Therapy. https://roamerstherapy.com/understanding-grief-a-journey-of-adaptation/

9. BetterHelp Editorial Team. (2025, February 27). *The Psychology Of The Grief Process: What Does Healthy Grief Look Like?*. BetterHelp. https://www.betterhelp.com/advice/grief/the-psychology-of-the-grief-process-what-does-healthy-grief-look-like/

10. Mnich, K.. (2025, September 5). *5 Stages of Grief: The Kübler-Ross Model*. PositivePsychology.com. https://positivepsychology.com/grief-stages/

11. The Supportive Care. (n.d.). *The Healing Process: How Grief Changes Over Time*. The Supportive Care. https://www.thesupportivecare.com/blog/the-healing-process-how-grief-changes-over-time

12. Friedman, R.. (2012, January 5). *Stages of Grief: The Myth*. Grief Recovery Method. https://www.griefrecoverymethod.com/blog/2012/01/stages-grief-myth

13. Flesner, J. M.. (2013). *A Shift in the Conceptual Understanding of Grief: Using Meaning-Oriented Therapies with Bereaved Clients*. Counseling Nexus: ACA's Digital Press. https://manifold.counseling.org/read/a-shift-in-the-conceptual-understanding-of-grief-using-meaning-oriented-therapies-with-bereaved-clients

14. Coleman, R. A., & Neimeyer, R. A.. (2010, October). *Measuring Meaning: Searching For and Making Sense of Spousal Loss in Late-Life*. PubMed Central. https://pmc.ncbi.nlm.nih.gov/articles/PMC3910232/

15. Klugman, C.. (2024, July 1). *Griefbots Are Here, Raising Questions of Privacy and Well-being*. The Hastings Center. https://www.thehastingscenter.org/griefbots-are-here-raising-questions-of-privacy-and-well-being/

16. Hussey, M.. (n.d.). *Talking to the dead: What happens when we bring back loved ones using AI*. The Brink - Improve Your Mental Health. https://www.thebrink.me/talking-to-the-dead-what-happens-when-we-bring-back-loved-ones-using-ai/

17. McGuire, C.. (2025, November 18). *AI Grief Companion: Why a Digital Twin of the Dead Can Be Ethical and Useful*. Swiss Institute of Artificial Intelligence. https://siai.org/memo/2025/11/202511283809

18. Kurzweil, A., & Story, D.. (2025, February 21). *We can now create compelling experiences of talking with our dead. Is this ghoulish, therapeutic or something else again?*. Aeon. https://aeon.co/essays/are-chatbots-of-the-dead-a-brilliant-idea-or-a-terrible-one

19. SuttaCentral. (n.d.). *AI now lets you talk to the dead*. SuttaCentral. https://discourse.suttacentral.net/t/ai-now-lets-you-talk-to-the-dead/38865

20. Krueger, J., & Osler, L.. (n.d.). *Communing with the Dead Online: Chatbots, Grief, and Continuing Bonds*. PhilArchive. https://philarchive.org/archive/KRUCWT

21. Hartmann, J.. (2025, August 10). *Evolutionary Psychology: Understanding Social Behavior Through a Cognitive Lens*. Oxfordshire Record Society. https://oxfordshire-record-society.org.uk/evolutionary-psychology-understanding-social-behavior-through-a-cognitive-lens/

22. Braren, S.. (2024, May 24). *The Evolution of Social Connection as a Basic Human Need*. The Social Creatures. https://www.thesocialcreatures.org/thecreaturetimes/evolution-of-social-connection

23. Petersen, M. B., Sznycer, D., Cosmides, L., & Tooby, J.. (2012, May 28). *Who Deserves Help? Evolutionary Psychology, Social Emotions, and Public Opinion about Welfare*. PubMed Central. https://pmc.ncbi.nlm.nih.gov/articles/PMC3551585/

24. Hartmann, J.. (2025, August 10). *Impact of Evolutionary Psychology on Society: Understanding Behaviour, Relationships, and Cultural Evolution*. NCMN. https://ncmn.ca/impact-of-evolutionary-psychology-on-society-understanding-behavior-relationships-and-cultural-evolution/

25. ResearchPod. (2025, February 26). *Size matters: The link between social groups and human evolution with Robin Dunbar*. ResearchPod. https://researchpod.org/behavioural-sciences/size-matters-social-groups-human-evolution

26. Gagliardi, M.. (2022, September 15). *Human attachment as a multi-dimensional control system: A computational implementation*. Frontiers in Psychology. https://pmc.ncbi.nlm.nih.gov/articles/PMC9521434/

27. Petters, D. (2019). *The attachment control system and computational modeling: Origins and prospects*. Developmental Psychology, 55(2), 227–239. **https://psycnet.apa.org/doiLanding?doi=10.1037%2Fdev0000647**

28. Mikulincer, M., & Shaver, P. R. (2007). *Attachment in Adulthood: Structure, Dynamics, and Change*. New York: Guilford Press.

29. K. G., A., & Joseph, J.. (2025, November 17). *The compassion illusion: Can artificial empathy ever be emotionally authentic?*. Frontiers in Psychology. https://pmc.ncbi.nlm.nih.gov/articles/PMC12665657/

30. Sustainability Directory. (2025, March 19). *Why Is Emotional Authenticity Threatened by Ai Interactions?*. Sustainability Directory. https://lifestyle.sustainability-directory.com/question/why-is-emotional-authenticity-threatened-by-ai-interactions/

31. O'Connor, M. F. (2019). *The Grieving Brain: The Surprising Science of How We Learn from Love and Loss.* HarperOne.

32. Feldman, R. (2017). The neurobiology of human attachments. *Trends in Cognitive Sciences.* https://doi.org/10.1016/j.tics.2017.03.005

33. Porges, S. W. (2011). *The Polyvagal Theory: Neurophysiological Foundations of Emotions, Attachment, Communication, and Self-Regulation.* W. W. Norton.

34. Friston, K. (2010). The free-energy principle: A unified brain theory? *Nature Reviews Neuroscience.* https://doi.org/10.1038/nrn2787

35. Clark, A. (2013). Whatever next? Predictive brains, situated agents, and the future of cognitive science. *Behavioral and Brain Sciences.* https://doi.org/10.1017/S0140525X12000477

36. Schacter, D. L., & Addis, D. R. (2007). The cognitive neuroscience of constructive memory: Remembering the past and imagining the future. *Philosophical Transactions of the Royal Society B.* https://doi.org/10.1098/rstb.2007.2087

37. Eisenberger, N. I., & Lieberman, M. D. (2004). Why rejection hurts: A common neural alarm system for physical and social pain. *Trends in Cognitive Sciences.* https://doi.org/10.1016/j.tics.2004.05.010 (doi.org in Bing)

38. Kross, E., Berman, M. G., Mischel, W., Smith, E. E., & Wager, T. D. (2011). Social rejection shares somatosensory representations with physical pain. *Proceedings of the National Academy of Sciences.* https://doi.org/10.1073/pnas.1102693108

39. Craig, A. D. (2009). How do you feel—now? The anterior insula and human awareness. *Nature Reviews Neuroscience.* https://doi.org/10.1038/nrn2555

40. Panksepp, J. (1998). *Affective Neuroscience: The Foundations of Human and Animal Emotions.* Oxford University Press.

41. Addis, D. R., Wong, A. T., & Schacter, D. L. (2007). Remembering the past and imagining the future: Common and distinct neural substrates. *Neuropsychologia.* https://doi.org/10.1016/j.neuropsychologia.2007.07.010

42. Berridge, K. C., & Kringelbach, M. L. (2015). Pleasure systems in the brain. *Neuron.* https://doi.org/10.1016/j.neuron.2015.02.018

43. Carter, C. S. (2014). Oxytocin pathways and the evolution of human behavior. *Annual Review of Psychology.* https://doi.org/10.1146/annurev-psych-010213-115110

44. O'Connor, M. F., Wellisch, D. K., Stanton, A. L., Eisenberger, N. I., Irwin, M. R., & Lieberman, M. D. (2008). Craving love? Enduring grief activates brain's reward center. *NeuroImage.* https://doi.org/10.1016/j.neuroimage.2008.06.040

45. University of Birmingham. (2026, January 23). *Who owns our digital afterlife? Helping the law keep pace with society.* University of Birmingham. https://www.birmingham.ac.uk/news/2026/who-owns-our-digital-afterlife-and-how-the-law-responds

46. Adams, N.-R.. (2024, September 24). *The digital afterlife: a guide to digital wills and legacies.* ITLawCo. https://itlawco.com/the-digital-afterlife-a-guide-to-digital-wills-and-legacies/

47. Alexander Holburn Beaudin + Lang LLP. (n.d.). *Your Digital Afterlife: Considerations for Estate Planning in the Cyberspace.* Alexander Holburn Beaudin + Lang LLP. https://www.ahbl.ca/your-digital-afterlife-considerations-for-estate-planning-in-the-cyberspace/

48. University of Birmingham. (n.d.). *Who Owns Our Digital Afterlife*. The Chronicle of Higher Education. https://www.chronicle.com/paid-content/university-of-birmingham/who-owns-our-digital-afterlife

49. Lindemann, N. F.. (2022, November 22). *The Ethics of 'Deathbots'*. PubMed Central. https://pmc.ncbi.nlm.nih.gov/articles/PMC9684218/

50. Dingman, S.. (2026, February 2). *As responses to death shift, this author is keeping an open mind about AI 'grief bots'*. KJZZ. https://www.kjzz.org/the-show/2026-02-02/as-responses-to-death-shift-this-author-is-keeping-an-open-mind-about-ai-grief-bots

51. Pacheco Flores, A.. (n.d.). *Grief Bot*. Spark: The magazine of Humanities Washington. https://www.humanities.org/spark/artificial-intelligence-death-grief/

52. Zohny, H.. (2025, January 29). *The Specter of Corporate Necromancy: Who Controls the Dead in the Age of Digital Doppelgängers?*. PubMed Central. https://pmc.ncbi.nlm.nih.gov/articles/PMC11789697/

53. Donnelly, S.. (2025, August 27). *AI Afterlife Avatars: $118B Market Growth and Ethical Challenges*. WebProNews. https://www.webpronews.com/ai-afterlife-avatars-118b-market-growth-and-ethical-challenges/

54. Erdener, J.. (2025, August 26). *Commodifying death: Thanatechnologies as platform workers in the digital afterlife economy*. New Media & Society. https://journals.sagepub.com/doi/10.1177/14614448251366173

55. StudyFinds Analysis. (2024, May 09). *Unethical 'deadbots' could exploit grieving families with ads using their loved one's face*. StudyFinds. https://studyfinds.org/deadbots-exploit-grieving-ads/

56. MDTech. (2024, May 15). *Digital Afterlife Industry | Myriad Digital*. Myriad Digital. https://mdgp.co.uk/tag/digital-afterlife-industry/

57. Metcalf, P., & Huntington, R. (1991). *Celebrations of Death: The Anthropology of Mortuary Ritual.* Cambridge University Press.

58. Bloch, M., & Parry, J. (1982). *Death and the Regeneration of Life.* Cambridge University Press.

59. Hertz, R. (1907/1960). A contribution to the study of the collective representation of death. *Sociological Review Monograph.*

60. Walter, T. (2015). New mourners, old mourners: Online memorial culture. *Bereavement Care.*

61. Kasket, E. (2012). Continuing bonds in the age of social networking: Facebook as a modern tool for the bereaved. *Bereavement Care.*

62. Brubaker, J. R., Hayes, G. R., & Dourish, P. (2013). Beyond the grave: Facebook as a site for the expansion of death and mourning. *The Information Society.*

63. Klass, D., Silverman, P. R., & Nickman, S. (1996). *Continuing Bonds: New Understandings of Grief.* Taylor & Francis.

64. Rosenblatt, P. C. (2008). Grief across cultures: A review and research agenda. *Omega: Journal of Death and Dying.*

65. Pintchman, T. (2005). *Guests at God's Wedding: Celebrating Kartik among the Women of Benares.* SUNY Press.

66. Lafleur, W. (1983). *The Karma of Words: Buddhism and the Literary Arts in Medieval Japan.* University of California Press.

67. Santino, J. (2006). Performative commemoratives: Spontaneous shrines and the public memorialization of death. *Folk Life.*

68. Park, J. (2010). Ancestor worship and ritual continuity in Korea. *Korean Journal of Religious Studies.*

69. Valentine, C. (2008). *Bereavement Narratives: Continuing Bonds in the Twenty-First Century.* Routledge.

70. Davies, D. (2002). *Death, Ritual and Belief: The Rhetoric of Funerary Rites.* Continuum.

71. Floridi, L. (2013). The ethics of information. *Oxford University Press.*

72. Öhman, C., & Floridi, L. (2017). The political economy of death in the age of information. *Minds and Machines.*

73. Stokes, P. (2015). Ghosts in the machine: Do the dead live on in Facebook. *Philosophy and Technology.*

74. Coeckelbergh, M. (2020). AI ethics. *MIT Press.*

75. Sri Takshara, K., & Bhuvaneswari, G.. (2025, June 26). *The role of death technologies in grief: an interdisciplinary examination of AI, cognition, and human expression.* Frontiers in Human Dynamics. https://www.frontiersin.org/journals/human-dynamics/articles/10.3389/fhumd.2025.1582914/full

76. Jia, S., Chi, O. H., & Tseng, H.. (n.d.). *AI-Driven Grief Chatbots: Transforming Grief Management for Individuals with Chronic Illness.* ScholarSpace at University of Hawaii at Manoa. https://scholarspace.manoa.hawaii.edu/server/api/core/bitstreams/e0b4f8c1-3d54-4821-a9fa-72275f32e991/content

77. Fu, M., Xiao, H., Ruan, H., Lin, Y., & Dong, X.. (2025, December 10). *Grieving in virtual worlds: emotional processes and generational differences in avatar-based memorials on VRChat.* Frontiers in Psychology. https://pmc.ncbi.nlm.nih.gov/articles/PMC12727626/

78. Thompson, S.. (2025, November 29). *Grief App vs Therapy: Why Digital Tools Complement Human Support*. Ahead. https://ahead-app.com/blog/grief/grief-app-vs-therapy-why-digital-tools-complement-human-support

79. Finucane, A.. (2024, October 15). *A rapid review of the evidence for online interventions for bereavement support*. PubMed Central. https://pmc.ncbi.nlm.nih.gov/articles/PMC11673319/

80. Thompson, S.. (2025, September 1). *Grief Apps vs. Human Connection: What the Research Actually Shows*. Ahead. https://ahead-app.com/blog/Grief/grief-apps-vs-human-connection-what-the-research-actually-shows

81. Yang, N., & Khanna, G. J.. (2025, May). *AI and Technology in Grief Support: Clinical Implications and Ethical Considerations*. The Counseling Psychologist. https://journals.sagepub.com/doi/abs/10.1177/00110000251352568

82. Stroebe, M., Schut, H., & Boerner, K. (2017). *Cautioning health-care professionals: Bereavement in the digital age*. Omega: Journal of Death and Dying, 74(4), 455–473

83. Klass, D., Silverman, P. R., & Nickman, S. L.. (1996). *Continuing Bonds: New Understandings of Grief – Death Education, Aging and Health Care. https://blackwells.co.uk/bookshop/product/9781560323396*

84. Parting Stone Editors. (n.d.). *The 3 C's of grief are Control, Connection, and Continuity*. Parting Stone Blog. https://blog.partingstone.com/what-are-the-3-cs-of-grief/

85. National Center for Biotechnology Information. (n.d.). *Interviewing the Internalized Other: An Introduction to the Method*. PubMed. https://pubmed.ncbi.nlm.nih.gov/21375121/

86. Banks, J.. (2024, August 1). *Deletion, departure, death: Experiences of AI companion loss.* Journal of Social and Personal Relationships. https://journals.sagepub.com/doi/10.1177/02654075241269688

87. With Grace. (n.d.). *How AI Can Support Grieving Children and Adults.* Funerals With Grace. https://funeralswithgrace.com/guide/ai-supporting-grieving-children-adults/

88. Schuurman, D. C.. (June 26, 2025). *Artificial Intelligence and Grief.* AI and Faith. https://aiandfaith.org/insights/artificial-intelligence-and-grief/

89. Harrell, E. (2021). *Identity Theft Victimization, 2018–2020.* U.S. Department of Justice, Bureau of Justice Statistics.

90. Kirchheimer, S. (2012). *Identity Theft of the Deceased: The High-Risk Nature of Post-Mortem Data.* Journal of Financial Crime, 19(3), 249–260.

91. Federal Trade Commission. (2023). *Protecting Deceased Loved Ones From Identity Theft.* FTC Consumer Advice.

92. National Alliance for Grieving Children. (n.d.). *Introduction to Grief Support Series | Grief-Tech: The Intersection of Grief and Technology.* NACG. https://nacg.org/resources_directory/grief-tech-intersection-of-grief-and-technology/

93. PESI Inc.. (n.d.). *The 2026 Grief Summit.* PESI. https://www.pesi.com/sales/bhs0023062026griefsummitorganic-1809332

94. Funeral.com, Inc.. (2026, January 26). *Grief Tech: The Best Apps for Storing Memories in 2026 (Privacy-First Options Included).* Funeral.com . https://funeral.com/blogs/the-journal/grief-tech-the-best-apps-for-storing-memories-in-2026-privacy-first-options-included

95. Vossel, H.. (2026, January 08). *Uncovering International Gaps in Bereavement Care*. Hospice News. https://hospicenews.com/2026/01/08/uncovering-international-gaps-in-bereavement-care/

96. Leong, E. R.. (2024, May 13). *Artificial intelligence 'ghost-bots' and the Christian understanding of death*. America Magazine. https://www.americamagazine.org/faith/2024/05/13/artificial-intelligence-bots-death-christianity-247885/

97. Henrickson, L. (2023, January 22). *Lifeworlds of the dead: Project December and the rhetoric, everyday experiences, and emotions of thanabots*. Media, Culture & Society. https://journals.sagepub.com/doi/10.1177/01634437221147626

www.ingramcontent.com/pod-product-compliance
Ingram Content Group UK Ltd.
Pitfield, Milton Keynes, MK11 3LW, UK
UKHW020143250726
13967UKWH00002B/835

9 781764 434720